First World War
and Army of Occupation
War Diary
France, Belgium and Germany

63 (ROYAL NAVAL) DIVISION
189 Infantry Brigade
Nelson Battalion
1 June 1916 - 23 February 1918

WO95/3114/3

The Naval & Military Press Ltd
www.nmarchive.com
Published in association with The National Archives

Published by

The Naval & Military Press Ltd

Unit 10 Ridgewood Industrial Park,
Uckfield, East Sussex,
TN22 5QE England
Tel: +44 (0) 1825 749494

www.naval-military-press.com

www.nmarchive.com

This diary has been reprinted in facsimile from the original. Any imperfections are inevitably reproduced and the quality may fall short of modern type and cartographic standards.

© **Crown Copyright**
Images reproduced by permission of The National Archives, London, England, 2015.

Contents

Document type	Place/Title	Date From	Date To
Heading	WO95/3114-3		
Heading	63rd (RN) Division 189th Infy Bde Nelson Battalion Jun 1916-Feb 1918		
Heading	June 1916 Nelson Bn Vol 1.		
Miscellaneous	War Diary of Nelson Battn From June 1st To June 30th Inclusive		
War Diary	Huppy	01/06/1916	02/06/1916
War Diary	En Route	03/06/1916	03/06/1916
War Diary	Beugin	04/06/1916	17/06/1916
War Diary	Verdrel	18/06/1916	21/06/1916
Heading	War Diary of "Nelson."B" 189th. Infantry Brigade 63rd R.N. Division From July 1st 1916 To July 31st 1916 Volume 2.		
War Diary	Hersin	01/07/1916	01/07/1916
War Diary	Trenches	02/07/1916	04/07/1916
War Diary	Verdrel	05/07/1916	05/07/1916
War Diary	Camblain Chatelain	05/07/1916	14/07/1916
War Diary	Coupigny Fosse 10	15/07/1916	19/07/1916
War Diary	Aix Noulette	20/07/1916	24/07/1916
War Diary	Sovehez II	25/07/1916	31/07/1916
Heading	War Diary of Nelson Battalion From 1st August 1916 To 31st August 1916		
War Diary	Bois De Noulette R 27 B 50	01/08/1916	07/08/1916
War Diary	Souchez II	07/08/1916	13/08/1916
War Diary	Bois De Noulette	13/08/1916	14/08/1916
War Diary	Ablain St Nazaire	15/08/1916	17/08/1916
War Diary	Souchez II	18/08/1916	24/08/1916
War Diary	Ablain St Nazaire	25/08/1916	31/08/1916
Heading	War Diary of Nelson Battalion From 1st September 1916 To 30 September 1916		
War Diary	Souchez II	01/09/1916	05/09/1916
War Diary	Lorette Spur	06/09/1916	06/09/1916
War Diary	Noulette Wood	07/09/1916	12/09/1916
War Diary	Souchez II	13/09/1916	18/09/1916
War Diary	Verdrel	19/09/1916	20/09/1916
War Diary	Magnicourt	21/09/1916	27/09/1916
War Diary	Bethonsart	28/09/1916	30/09/1916
Heading	War Diary of Nelson Battalion 189th Infy Bgde. 63rd R.N. Division From 1 October 1916 To 31 October 1916		
War Diary	Bethonsart	01/10/1916	04/10/1916
War Diary	Acheux	05/10/1916	08/10/1916
War Diary	Engle Belmer	09/10/1916	16/10/1916
War Diary	Auchon Villers Sector	17/10/1916	17/10/1916
War Diary	Engle Belmer.	18/10/1916	20/10/1916
War Diary	Mesnil	21/10/1916	21/10/1916
War Diary	Hamel	22/10/1916	24/10/1916
War Diary	Englebelmer	25/10/1916	31/10/1916

Heading	War Diary of Nelson Battalion 189th Infy. Bgde 63rd. R.N. Division From 1st November 1916 To 30th November 1916		
War Diary	Puchvillers	01/11/1916	06/11/1916
War Diary	Engle Belmer	07/11/1916	08/11/1916
War Diary	Hamel Left Sector	09/11/1916	10/11/1916
War Diary	Engle Belmer	11/11/1916	12/11/1916
War Diary	Hamel Sector	13/11/1916	19/11/1916
War Diary	Candas	20/11/1916	24/11/1916
War Diary	Le Champneut	25/11/1916	30/11/1916
Operation(al) Order(s)	Nelson Battalion Order 50	25/10/1916	25/10/1916
Miscellaneous	Time Table To Be Used In Connection With Barrage Table.		
War Diary	Nelson Battalion Order No. 51.	27/10/1916	27/10/1916
Heading	War Diary of Nelson Battalion From December 1st 1916 To December 31st 1916.		
War Diary	Le Champneut	01/12/1916	17/12/1916
War Diary	Champneut	18/12/1916	31/12/1916
Heading	War Diary of Nelson Battalion 189th Brigade 63rd R.N. Division From 1st December 1916 To January 1917		
War Diary	Le Champneut	01/01/1917	14/01/1917
War Diary	Gapennes	15/01/1917	15/01/1917
War Diary	Candas	16/01/1917	17/01/1917
War Diary	Rubempre	18/01/1917	18/01/1917
War Diary	Beaucourt (Left)	19/01/1917	22/01/1917
War Diary	Beaucourt (Support)	23/01/1917	27/01/1917
Heading	War Diary of Nelson Battn-189th. Bdg. 63rd. RN. Div. From 1st February 1917 To 28th February 1917		
War Diary	Beaucourt	01/02/1917	10/02/1917
War Diary	Englebelmer	10/02/1917	11/02/1917
War Diary	Lealvillers	11/02/1917	12/02/1917
War Diary	Thiepval	13/02/1917	18/02/1917
War Diary	Forceville	13/02/1917	13/02/1917
War Diary	Lealvillers	13/02/1917	17/02/1917
War Diary	Thiepval	18/02/1917	18/02/1917
War Diary	Forceville	18/02/1917	18/02/1917
War Diary	Lealvillers	18/02/1917	18/02/1917
War Diary	Hedauville	19/02/1917	24/02/1917
War Diary	Thiepval	25/02/1917	25/02/1917
War Diary	Hedauville	25/02/1917	25/02/1917
War Diary	Varennes	25/02/1917	26/02/1917
War Diary	Thiepval	27/02/1917	27/02/1917
War Diary	Poz	27/02/1917	28/02/1917
Miscellaneous	Nelson Battalion, 63rd., (R.N.) Division.	01/02/1917	01/02/1917
Operation(al) Order(s)	Operation Order No. 7 by Commander E.W. Nelson RNVR., Commanding Nelson Battalion	02/02/1917	02/02/1917
Miscellaneous	O.C., No. 3 Battalion. Appendix 2.		
Miscellaneous	Defence Scheme	05/02/1917	05/02/1917
War Diary	Report on Lewis Guns damaged during Operations. Appendix 4		
Heading	War Diary of Nelson Battalion, 189th. Infantry Brigade 63rd. (Royal Naval) Division From 1st. March 1917 To 31st. March 1917		
War Diary	Spring Garden Camp	01/03/1917	26/03/1917
War Diary	Annezin	27/03/1917	31/03/1917

Heading	War Diary of Nelson Battalion. 189 Infantry Brigade 63rd (Royal Naval) Division From 1st April 1917 To 30 April 1917		
War Diary	Annezin	01/04/1917	07/04/1917
War Diary	Ruitz	08/04/1917	11/04/1917
War Diary	Villers. Brulin	12/04/1917	12/04/1917
War Diary	Ecoivres	13/04/1917	25/04/1917
War Diary	Maroeuil	26/04/1917	27/04/1917
War Diary	Villers Brulin	28/04/1917	29/04/1917
War Diary	Beugin	30/04/1917	30/04/1917
Heading	War Diary of Nelson Batt-189th Bdg 63rd R.N. Division From 1st May 1917 To 31st May 1917		
War Diary	Beugin	01/05/1917	04/05/1917
War Diary	Old Roman Trenches G.b.6.	05/05/1917	08/05/1917
War Diary	Old German Trenches (G.6.b) (51B NW)	09/05/1917	20/05/1917
War Diary	St Catherine G.15.a.	21/05/1917	23/05/1917
War Diary	Rocklincourt Arras Rd G.5.a (Wakefield Camp)	25/05/1917	31/05/1917
Heading	War Diary of Nelson Battn.-189th Infantry Brigade 63rd (Royal Naval) Division From 1st June 1917 To 30th June 1917		
War Diary	Rocklincourt Arras Road Wakefield Camp	01/06/1917	01/06/1917
War Diary	Battn In Support At B,21,c (Bailleul)	02/06/1917	04/06/1917
War Diary	Front Line Opposite Copy	05/06/1917	10/06/1917
War Diary	Rocklincourt	11/06/1917	11/06/1917
War Diary	A28.a.6.4	12/06/1917	12/06/1917
War Diary	G6C.54 Old German Line	13/06/1917	13/06/1917
War Diary	Rocklincourt G.4.c.54 Old German Line	15/06/1917	21/06/1917
War Diary	Maroeuil F27B6.3 (51.G.N.E.)	22/06/1917	30/06/1917
Heading	War Diary of Nelson Battalion 189th Infantry Brigade From 1st July 1917 To 31st July 1917.		
War Diary	Maroeuil E 27 B 6-3 51 C N E	01/07/1917	03/07/1917
War Diary	Left Support Battn Sugar Post NW. B 51 B 16d	04/07/1917	09/07/1917
War Diary	Front Line N.A Dpry B.12.	10/07/1917	18/07/1917
War Diary	Wakefield Camp 51 B N.W. A 21.c 5.8.	19/07/1917	30/07/1917
War Diary	Bois De la Maison Blanche H 1.c.67	31/07/1917	07/08/1917
War Diary	Maison Blanche Left Sub Sector Div Front	07/08/1917	13/08/1917
War Diary	Left Sub Sector Div Front	13/08/1917	16/08/1917
War Diary	Aubrey Camp	17/08/1917	23/08/1917
War Diary	Right Subsector	24/08/1917	29/08/1917
War Diary	Naval Trench	30/08/1917	31/08/1917
War Diary	War Diary From 1st September 1917 To 30th September, 1917		
War Diary	Naval Trench	01/09/1917	01/09/1917
War Diary	Railway Cutting	02/09/1917	04/09/1917
War Diary	R4. Sub Sec.	05/09/1917	10/09/1917
War Diary	Maroeuil	11/09/1917	11/09/1917
War Diary	Aubrey Camp	12/09/1917	16/09/1917
War Diary	Roundhay Camp	17/09/1917	25/09/1917
War Diary	Tinques	25/09/1917	30/09/1917
Heading	Nelson Battalion. War Diary From 1st October, 1917 To 31st October 1917		
War Diary	Tincques	01/10/1917	03/10/1917
War Diary	Nouveau Monde	04/10/1917	06/10/1917
War Diary	Reigersburg	06/10/1917	12/10/1917
War Diary	Kempton Park	13/10/1917	19/10/1917
War Diary	La Brique Camp	20/10/1917	23/10/1917

War Diary	Brake Camp.	24/10/1917	31/10/1917
Heading	War Diary From 1st November 1917 To 30th November 1917		
War Diary	South Of Spriet	01/11/1917	03/11/1917
War Diary	Canal Bank	04/11/1917	05/11/1917
War Diary	Road Camp	06/11/1917	10/11/1917
War Diary	Winnezeele	11/11/1917	11/11/1917
War Diary	Helsthaege	12/11/1917	29/11/1917
War Diary	Road Camp.	30/11/1917	09/12/1917
War Diary	L Camp Barastre	10/12/1917	10/12/1917
War Diary	Barastre	11/12/1917	11/12/1917
War Diary	Etricourt	12/12/1917	28/12/1917
War Diary	Highland Ridge Ref. Nine Wood. 1/10,000. Sht.57c.	29/12/1917	29/12/1917
War Diary	Operations In Counter Attack.	30/12/1917	31/12/1917
War Diary	In The Line-La. Vacquerie Sector.	01/01/1918	06/01/1918
War Diary	Metz	07/01/1918	08/01/1918
War Diary	In The Line	09/01/1918	10/01/1918
War Diary	Nelson Camp [Havrincourt Wood	11/01/1918	17/01/1918
War Diary	In The Line	18/01/1918	21/01/1918
War Diary	Havrincourt Wood	21/01/1918	21/01/1918
War Diary	Equancourt	22/01/1918	22/01/1918
War Diary	Barastre Area.	23/01/1918	29/01/1918
War Diary	Camp. 0.10c. 39. Ref. Sht 57C SW 1/40,000.	30/01/1918	31/01/1918
Heading	Final War Diary of The Nelson Battalion From 1st February 1918 To 28th February 1918		
War Diary	Barastre Area Camp O.10c.39.Ref.sht.57c. S.W. 1/40,000	01/02/1918	13/02/1918
War Diary	Barastre Area	14/02/1918	23/02/1918

WD95/3114(3)

WD95/3114(3)

63RD (RN) DIVISION
189TH INFY BDE

NELSON BATTALION
JUN 1916 – FEB 1918

Disbanded

June 1946
Nelson Bn
Vol 1.

"Confidential"

Headquarters "NELSON" Bⁿ
R.N.D.
July 2ⁿᵈ 1916.

WAR DIARY
OF
NELSON BATTⁿ
from
June 1ˢᵗ
to
June 30ᵗʰ inclusive.

RoBurge
Lᵗ Col R.M.L.I.
O.C. "Nelson" Bⁿ R.N.D.

To The
A.G's Office.
3ʳᵈ Echelon.

WAR DIARY

PLACE	DATE	HOUR	SUMMARY OF EVENTS	REMARKS ETC
HUPPY	June 1st	—	Batt⁰ in Billets. Fitting up with Motor Stores etc	
"	" 2nd	2000	Received orders from 2nd R.N.Bde to leave at 07:00 # 3rd unit to proceed to IV Army Training Area	
En route	" 3rd		Appeared an ordered at PONT REMY STN at 1000 for 1030 train. Train finally left 1340. Arrived BRIAS 1805. Marched to BEUGIN arriving 2200. Much unnecessary hardship & discomfort to men owing to alteration of hours resulting in haversack ration only between 0530 and 2200.	
BEUGIN	" 4th		Cleaning up billets which were very dirty and insanitary. Latrines, refuse pits etc left open by last occupants.	
"	" 5th		Cleaning billets & wash. clothes. Signal from 1st Army to wire fighting strength to 1st Army & repeat IV Corps. Reply 25 Offrs 735 OR. C/sios of whole to 2nd R.N.BDE.	
"	" 6th		V.Wet. (M) Lectures, Intervals for Summer clothing, etc. No work outside billets.	
"	" 7th		Company Route marches. Specialists under instruction	
"	" 8th		Batt⁰ at shower baths. Remainder of time Musketry instruction	
"	" 9th		Snipers at 30" range. (M) Route marches. Specialists under instruction. Cov/sits IV Army School	
"	" 10th		One Coy on range (30") Remainder as requisite. Specialists under inst.	
"	" 11th		Sunday. 11 Offrs + 49 OR to various schools of instruction	

WAR DIARY

Place	Date	Hour	Summary of Events	Remarks etc.
BEUGIN	June 12th	—	Two Coys grouping on 30x range. Double Company route march. Lecture on Trench discipline by Brigadier. 7 Offrs and 55 OR left for Schools of Instruction. Specialists under Instruction. Remainder Drill under 2nd I/C	
"	13th	"	ditto . 1 Coy at 30x range	
"	14th	"	ditto	
"	15th	"	One Coy Snipers & bombers at 30x range. Sigs under instruction. Remainder digging trenches at Brigade Bomb School. 2 Offrs 75 OR rejoined from MARSEILLES.	
"	16th	"	Detail of work as for 15th:	
"	17th	"	Work as above. 4 pm Received orders to move to VERDREL. "B" moved off 5.15 pm arrived 8.0 pm. Transport arrived 9 pm. Barbwr & Sigs left at BEUGIN	
VERDREL	18th	"	(Sunday) 6 am. 1 Off + 50 OR for Working Party. 3.30 pm. 30 Offs + 500 OR dfts	
"	19th	"	Party of 500 no store returned midnight 18/19 not new required. 1 Coy Musical Inspection for skin diseases. 1 Coy Gas Lecture 2 Coys Drill	
"	20th	"	Forenoon Coys under instruction. Afft. Strong easy for all night Working Party. 14 offrs 250 OR 2 pm Received orders prepare move to HERSIN tomorrow. 5 pm Move orders cancelled. Inspection for skin diseases completed.	
"	21st	"	7 am. Night working party returned. 10 Offrs 50 OR working party to MARQUEFFLES.	

Confidential

Head qr Nelson Batt'n
17/8/16

WAR DIARY

OF

"NELSON" Bn 189th INFANTRY BRIGADE 63rd R.N. DIVISION.

from

July 1st 1916.

to

July 31st 1916.

Volume I.

R J Burge
Lt Col R.M.L.I.
Cmdg "Nelson" Bn

Volume I.

To Hd Qrs
189th Inf. Bde.

63
Nelson Bn
1912
July

Army Form C. 2118.

WAR DIARY
or
INTELLIGENCE SUMMARY.
(Erase heading not required.)

Instructions regarding War Diaries and Intelligence Summaries are contained in F.S. Regs., Part II. and the Staff Manual respectively. Title pages will be prepared in manuscript.

Place	Date	Hour	Summary of Events and Information	Remarks and references to Appendices
HERSIN	1/July/1	2 pm	Jefferson A.T.B. Coy. I.H.Q. & where 22nd London Rif. in 1. sub-sect or ANGRES II. Strick had BULLY TRENCH 4 p.m. Relief complete 7 p.m. Dugouts A.T.B. in F.L. & C. Reserve. D attached to Battalion on right. Situation Normal.	
TRENCHES	2/July/2		Much repairing work in F.L. & Supports. Stokes mortars on working parties. Enemy active with Minenwerfer Grampnels & rifle grenades. Good deal of damage to our trenches.	
	3	9.45 p.m.	Opened fire right with Stokes guns (5) Medium TM's (4) Rifle Grenades (3) with previous selected strongpts. Rapid slow periods alternating for 3/4 hour. Enemy reply feeble mostly at our mortar positions from enemy active with rifle grenades. Replied with 40 rounds Stokes mortar. Enemy silenced.	
	4	1.30 am	In conjunction with raid further south, swept enemy's lines with Lewis Guns TM's Stokes Rifle Grenades.	
		4 till 5.30 am	Enemy reply weak on right but reasonable & well sustained on left particular near Berry Crater. During each night patrols were out & Lewis guns swept German enemy works. Enemy reported to list of his damage done. 7 pm Battalion relieved by 22nd London Regiment. Total casualties for period killed A. Wounds 17. Battalion proceeds to billets at VERDREL for night.	
VERDREL & BLAIN CHATELAIN	5/July/5		Left to officers, 672 O.R's at VERDREL for attachment to 2nd & 47th Divisions for instructing active HQ & remainder to CAMBLAIN CHATELAIN to billets. Arrived 7 pm.	May 7
BLAIN CHATELAIN	6		Gueridon up. Returned blankets & rail heads.	
	7		Moved Battalion here from Blaugin BEUGIN	

T.2134. Wt. W.708-776. 500000. 4/15. Sir J. C. & S.

WAR DIARY
or
INTELLIGENCE SUMMARY.

Army Form C. 2118.

(Erase heading not required.)

Instructions regarding War Diaries and Intelligence Summaries are contained in F. S. Regs., Part II. and the Staff Manual respectively. Title pages will be prepared in manuscript.

Place	Date	Hour	Summary of Events and Information	Remarks and references to Appendices
CAMBLAIN CHÂTELAIN	July/15		No medical of soldiers. Weather fine & warm	
	9		Lecture to all available officers on Trench Patrol Work by Canadian S.O. at FERMES	
	10		Working parties for Ohio. Also Officer of Co. (preparing orders) returned to Battalion.	Tres. reversed
	11	4pm	300 men passed through baths. Remainder of day moving clothing Co.	Showers
	12		Reorganization of Battn. for new establishment of Bn. HQ. Bombing platoon to & training	
	13		Above commenced for above. Also Snipers Scouts Bayonet fighting. Remainder instruction & clearing village	
	14		Battn. Specialists & Boys at training. Received orders to move	Weather
PIGNY	15		Marched to CUPANY (10 miles) to take up billets. Arrived 4.30 pm	Weather
SS 10	16		Marched to FOSSE 10 (2 miles) & took up billets. Arrived 7.30 pm	
	17		Sunday inspection. Lieut. Dupont & 16th (Officers & 50) returned Jan 16.	Scotch visit
	18		Specialists under instruction. Remainder at Bayonet fighting	Warm
	19		At 10.30pm Battalion march to MT. NOULETTE woods.	"
NOULETTE	20		General clearing up of billets. 150 men returned from working party 5 am. Total of 290 men proceeding on working parties.	

WAR DIARY or INTELLIGENCE SUMMARY

Army Form C. 2118.

Place	Date	Hour	Summary of Events and Information	Remarks and references to Appendices
X Nouel-ette	21 July		Night patrol nothing. 80 men on day W.P. Dug out party left 19th inst	Weather
	22.		Some buys W.P. 140 night W.P. Specialists under instruction	"
	23.		As above. On 21st/22nd/23rd parties of officers visiting South & Z II sub F.S.	
	24.		As above. Coy Comdr & 1 N.C.O. per platoon to take over trenches for a day	n.s.
Ouchts II	25.	9 pm	Battn. relieved HAWKE in trenches. Relief completed 12.30 am 26th. Ranges Sketches etc. 3 Coy in F.L. made with 2 platoons in support, 1 Coy in Reserve in Bois Sixe, other area of ARRAS ROAD.	
	26th		Commenced work chiefly drainage, wiring and strengthening of weak points. Aeroplane from enemy very slight.	
	27th		A great deal of work done in trenches. Nothing done in afternoon from 3.30 to 4.7 super enemy sniping very many	
			to strafe by our snipers. T.M.s and Artillery.	
	28.		Work continued as above. New O.P. Kommenceur little night work owing to fire from our own Batteries	
			Slight aeroplane view to trenches	
	29		Continued work as before. New enemy wire noticed opp. ROTTEN ROW	very foggy
	30		As above. Nothing of importance reported. Lewis Guns relieved by HAWKE	
	31		Slight aeroplane by heavy minenwerfer Retaliation from 18 pdr guns of enemy trenches (HAWK RE)	V. warm
			hand entered through wrist of officer 5'30". Returned portion of relieving Battn. (HAWK RE)	

Army Form C. 2118.

WAR DIARY
or
INTELLIGENCE SUMMARY.
(Erase heading not required.)

Instructions regarding War Diaries and Intelligence Summaries are contained in F. S. Regs., Part II. and the Staff Manual respectively. Title pages will be prepared in manuscript.

Place	Date	Hour	Summary of Events and Information	Remarks and references to Appendices
VERDUN	July 31		arrived at various times during day. Battalion relieved 11.35 pm & proceeded to Bois de Mortetir. Total Casualties during period 1 Killed 2 Wounded. Nothing Else.	

"Confidential"

HEADQUARTERS
NELSON BATTALION
31st August 1916

WAR DIARY

of

NELSON BATTALION

from

1st August 1916

to

31st August 1916

R. Burge
O/C. Nelson Battn.

To Headquarters
189th Infantry Brigade

WAR DIARY
or
INTELLIGENCE SUMMARY.
(Erase heading not required.)

Army Form C. 2118.

Nelson Battalion

Place	Date	Hour	Summary of Events and Information	Remarks and references to Appendices
Bois de Mons RTE R.27 b 60	Aug 1		Battalion inspected by M.O. 6 cases of scabies discovered. Manoeuvres. 150 on working parties at night	Very warm
	2		Instruction in afternoon especially Bayonet fighting. Working party 140	very warm
	3		Drill and Instruction in afternoon. Working parties 140	warm
	4		Gas drills issued to all men - bathing. Working parties 160	warm
	5		Officers rodes to relieve HAWKE Battalion in SOUCHEZ on night of August 6/7. Working parties 160	warm
	6		Officers & N.C.O.s to Andre C.R.M & NCO for Platoon in advance - guides at R.E. Dugout by R.N.D.D. and 2 cooks nr Qs to Base. Two officers & 16 Batchelor Mecklenburg to Base to understudy. Working 140/km Transport & Quarter Masters Department	
	6/7	9 pm	La Mr. relieved HAWKE in Touches I. Relief completed 11.35 pm (7th inst) HQr occupy whole of front line with 1 Company, attached for instruction "C" & "D" Coys in support "B" Coy has 2 Platoons in BAJOLLE. "A" Coy in BOIS SIX has 2 Platoons at "B".	fresh
Souchez I.	7		Commenced work - drainage KELLET, BOSCHE, STRAIGHT. New traverses in BOSCHE. Clearing trenches damaged previous afternoon by T.M. bombardment.	fair
		6 pm	Enemy fires 7/10 rounds Minenwerfer at junction HUN + KELLET, Med T. M.s (2) at HUN + LINK knocked out. Retaliation by T.N.s & Artillery	
	8		Working on both Coy fronts and 3 patrols out last night. Night quiet except for desultory sniping	

T2134. Wt. W708—770. 500000. 4/15. Str J.C. & S.

WAR DIARY
or
INTELLIGENCE SUMMARY

Army Form C. 2118.

Place	Date	Hour	Summary of Events and Information	Remarks and references to Appendices
DUCHEZ IV	1916 8		This morning an unsuspicious man shot by one of our snipers with a telescopic sight. In preparation for relief B Coy R.M.L.I. were attached to us by D Coy. B Coy were moved back to support trench. Minenwerfers have fired about 10 rounds between 6pm & 7pm but without doing any serious damage.	
	9		Wiring and Patrols as yesterday. A further portion of KELLET bdy damaged by Minnies. Artillery retaliation stopped this. Installed trench from Stone Building (S.16) opposite trench. Enemy Snipers shot in the forenoon. 2 Anti trench mortars between H.16 & F.L. Was similar number NELSONS to Support. Seven wounded.	
	10		Large number of men being all along front line although to be done still. One Coys Guns fired intermittently but made harassing fire in 1st midday enemy 2nd to man out parties per code. =Sniping about in reply to Minnie which stopped shortly after our artillery reach. Wiring Patrols as before. The enemy starting early with rifle grenades and carrying so later with shells & minnies were more active than usual (probable retaliation from artillery as necessary to stop this)	
	11		During retaliation one of our M.T. mortars fell in ROTTEN ROW killing 2 men and wounding 3 others (Unds Gnns Klmnuch by HAWKE	
	12		Bratt advanced parties of relieving battalion (HAWKE) arrived at various times during day. Battalion relieved reasonably and proceeded to AIX NOULETTE WOOD total casualties during trench period 1. Killed 14 wounded. (2 of which died of wounds)	

WAR DIARY
or
INTELLIGENCE SUMMARY.
(Erase heading not required.)

Army Form C. 2118.

Place	Date	Hour	Summary of Events and Information	Remarks and references to Appendices
BOIS DE NOULETTE	May 13		Patrolson visited by No. 19 Coast of sentries discovered. Batn had orders. Orders to move to LORETTE SPUR cancelled. 5 pm.	Pris.
	14		Instruction parties fighting and wiring. Marched to LORETTE SPUR relieving DRAKE Batn. Steps at ABLAIN ST NAZAIRE – Arrived 11.30 pm (¾ miles)	Mist.
ABLAIN ST NAZAIRE	15		Working Party of 2 officers & 100 O.Rs to Engineers	Mist.
	16		– 12.160 sent down to AIX NOULETTE to 3rd Field Coy Engineers. 6 Relief 12 already here.	Fine.
	17		Working Party as above. Rifle fire relieved HAWKE Batn from in SOUCHEZ I	Very heavy rain.
SOUCHEZ II	18		Marched & relieved HAWKE in SOUCHEZ II throughout the day. Battalion relief complete 12.30 a.m. 19th Disposition B C (69) on right, NELSON D Coy centre. A Coy left making F.L. + supports 2 platoons in B, & C Coy in BAJOLLE the other 2 platoons C Coy in MAROC. BOIS SIX	not.
	19		Commenced work on trenches chiefly drainages. Also carried on work on strong points. Construction of a new trench at junction Yprsman Road & BOSCHE WALK. Shared BOSCHE WALK above still had flares in sides. Our artillery bombarded enemy area between 4.15 and 4.30 pm. Arts good. Effect Salute and wiring as usual.	This
	20		Day mostly quiet. Took continued ordinary duties. Morning & Rifle grenades were sent over between	

T2134. Wt. W708–776. 500000. 4/15. Sir J. C. & S.

WAR DIARY
or
INTELLIGENCE SUMMARY.
(Erase heading not required.)

Army Form C. 2118.

Instructions regarding War Diaries and Intelligence Summaries are contained in F. S. Regs., Part II. and the Staff Manual respectively. Title pages will be prepared in manuscript.

Place	Date	Hour	Summary of Events and Information	Remarks and references to Appendices
BUCHEZ.	20		6.15 and 7 am in reply to several shots from our 60 pdr. Aff 10.30 am Gas was sent over by the battalion on our left and the enemy's trenches bombarded heavily. The reply in his lines was weak principally H.E. Shrapnel Rifle Grenade Stokes machines fire very active. Two rifle grenades reported to have fallen behind G. STRAIGHT. Two enemy machine guns reported in enemy second line about SW.32.b.21.	Two
	21		Apparently quiet – reports continues instruction and strong points and a deep latrine started also sanitary arrangements. Usual patrols and wiring carried out.	
	22		Enemy started bombarding round about HEAD QUARTERS Trench with A.Z howitzers firing on Hill 12.30 pm at intervals ceasing at 10.30 am. Rifle grenades were sent over on our left round at KELLY Station Retaliation stopped the rifle grenade firing. Enemy guns opened down a little under distincts retaliation from our artillery. 4.15 – 4.38 pm Artillery bombarded enemy area Retaliation very slight. 8.50 pm M.T.M. and T.M. fired the enemy's trenches 7.30 pm. Usual patrols wiring. Repairs carried out. Work done on Zshafts & new deep dugout in Roche WALK.	two
	23		Morning quiet but enemy became active with rifle grenades & minnies on our left in retaliation to release fire by our. Enemy quiet. Usual working parties & leave parties relieved.	release
	24	7-30 am	M.T.M. fired on enemy's trenches. Our They replied with minnies and more two Minnies	

WAR DIARY
or
INTELLIGENCE SUMMARY.
(Erase heading not required.)

Army Form C. 2118.

Place	Date	Hour	Summary of Events and Information	Remarks and references to Appendices
AUCHEZ	24		In afternoon between 2.30 pm & 3 pm 2" mortars again bombarded the retaliation was rifles strong. Rifle grenades slackened the fire and a few S.Q.S were also fired over 5 pm Hannescamps party of HAWKE Batt. arrived signalling Brigade S.O.S. Relief complete 11.30pm Battalion moved to Beaux Maroquin via LORETTE SPUR Batt. Hdqrs. ABLAIN ST NAZAIRE. Total casualties during trench tour - one wounded.	S.W.M
ABLAIN ST NAZAIRE	25		Working party 2 officers & 100 O.Rs. for Engineers and nightly officers patrol started to prevent enemy snooping in the open.	
	26		Working parties. Patrols as above. 1" additional 6 men working under Engineers laying duck boards in front line and 30 men working round Headquarters	wet
	27		Working parties as above - also patrol established between ABLAIN ST NAZAIRE shelled. About 6 shells falling shortly after 2 pm which did not explode. No casualties & no damage.	
	28		Working parties as above. Machine gun advice on control by during the night. Reinforcements arrived 6 (150 O.Rs including 4 Pos & 7 L.S.) posted to Coys A 33. B 43. C. 47. D 35". Signallers (Hdqrs) 3	wet
	29		March was interrupted by thunderstorm accompanied by heavy rain & guns returning to HAVRE	

Army Form C. 2118.

WAR DIARY
or
INTELLIGENCE SUMMARY.
(Erase heading not required.)

Place	Date	Hour	Summary of Events and Information	Remarks and references to Appendices
LMN 57 NAZARE	Aug 30		Battalion relieved HAWKE in SOUCHEZ I. Moved into transport lines - chief complaint rats.	
		12.30 am (31st)	Dispositions B Coy right C Coy left each Coy taking over 2 platoons. D Coy in support. Subsidiary junction of frontage of C & B Coys OP at South end of GERMAN ROAD. Listening posts out all night.	
	31		Medium TM's unable to fire having been arranged in afternoon from rifle grenades. Arrangements for repatriation Trench Mortar carriers on drainage throughout the lines. Lewis Guns fired on working party team.	

R.G.Burgess
Lt Col

CONFIDENTIAL.

Headquarters
Nelson Battⁿ
30 Sept 1916

WAR DIARY

of

NELSON BATTALION

from

1st September 1916

to

30 September 1916.

R^t Burge
Lt Col
I/C Nelson Battⁿ

WAR DIARY or INTELLIGENCE SUMMARY

Army Form C. 2118.

Place	Date	Hour	Summary of Events and Information	Remarks and references to Appendices
JUNEZ B.	Sept 1		Usual patrols & listening posts during night. 2" mortar club were on enemys front 1.30pm to 2.15pm and again from 6.15pm and only retaliation was the rifle grenade. One of our aeroplanes flew down the enemys lines very low, reported to be dropping handbills. Work on drainage and deep dugout continued. Casualties one other rank killed.	Fair
	2		Night was quiet. One enemy machine gun active on left sides. Stokes TM. opened deliberate fire on enemys trenches 8.45pm Slight retaliation. Fourteenth rifle grenades activity by us during the day. Grenadoes not grounded.	
	3		Enhanced activity with Lewis guns and machine guns on both sides, throughout the night. Trenches fired but. During afternoon our heavy artillery bombarded Kite Junction. There was no retaliation on our sector. Otherwise as usual. Casualties	Fine
	4		During the night Wary Straß on Nieu by Artillery. Enemy Howitzer about 12.3 grm was a few charges rifle. Co-damned. Same. Our 2" Trench Mortars fired on enemys line 7.45 P.B. 9am and also on afternoon activity. First mortar about 6.30pm. Patrol made useful observations of enemys trench on night. No casualties.	
	5		5 30am During early morning hours, fire was returned by Minnie Batr's. Morning quiet except for two stoney. much felt brand Pollis Greenhants church. Evening. Belts relief complete 12 midnight. Rest provided by 13 left to join Sin Bn for support line. LORETTE SPUR. Disposition Right Coys left Nice (one respectively). D. Coy left in lines S. Pr. Left or support line LORETTE NO: W. Hotel. Stay dug in, party of 3 a the left attached to D.Coy in order to carry on the work on the Boom way.	

WAR DIARY or INTELLIGENCE SUMMARY

Army Form C. 2118.

(Erase heading not required.)

Instructions regarding War Diaries and Intelligence Summaries are contained in F.S. Regs, Part II. and the Staff Manual respectively. Title pages will be prepared in manuscript.

Place	Date	Hour	Summary of Events and Information	Remarks and references to Appendices
SOUCHEZ	5		Work done during period in trenches O.My3 & My2ois BOSCHE WALK progressed. Satisfactorily as Company Patrol was throughout whole subsector. Casualties one OR wounded. Total casualties during trench period 1 OR killed & 2 OR wounded.	
NOULETTE WOOD	6		On night of 6/7 Battalion moved to NOULETTE WOOD.	Fine
NOULETTE WOOD	7		Make and mend. 2 off & 175 NCOs working parties. MO inspected Battalion. 8 cases of scabies discovered. A.& T.O. & baths & had clean shirts. L.Gn Bombers sent to Infantry School. 6 Major went through Baths and received clean shirts. Working parties of 75 ORs at night.	"
	8		3 Majors deep dugout party returned from BOIS SIX. 32 ORs. Permanent working party the NOULETTE returned 41 ORs. Working parties 95 ORs.	"
	9		Coys, Pros, Hos, & NCOs service talks. Working parties 95 ORs.	
	10		Working parties 95 ORs. Lewis guns (5 teams) relieving HAWKE Batt in SOUCHEZ II. 16 ORs left for General duty.	
	11		6 day Coy.	
	12		The NOULETTE guards relieved by HAWKE Batt during the day. Batt. relieved HAWKE in SOUCHEZ II. Hostile aircraft 10.50pm. Disposition A Coy support BULL Six. D Coy right B centre & left. B Coy in Nabron in GAZELLE LINE. Relief carried out by standing patrols.	Fine
SOUCHEZ II	13		Platoon of A Coy brought up to RELIEF from BAJOLLE in support & D Coy. Work progress - drainage etc.	

WAR DIARY
or
INTELLIGENCE SUMMARY.
(Erase heading not required.)

Army Form C. 2118.

Place	Date	Hour	Summary of Events and Information	Remarks and references to Appendices
CHEZ II	13.		By means of spirit trench Duckboards to whole of ROTTEN ROW. Drainage & general sanitation throughout has rather bad extinction of KELLET where it had been blown in. Slight minnie retaliation from 2" mortar fire supported by Stokes but no damage done. Lewis guns active during night patrols as usual. The enemy on our right brought slight retaliation on our lines during the night bring very little damage but 2 men were slightly wounded and one suffered from shell shock. Lewis guns active & patrols & listening posts as usual.	Fine
	14.			Showers
	15.		Day quiet slight retaliation trench mortar fire by minnies. Working during night Drawing retrench. Started to South of ASH ROAD with object of diverting minnies fire from junction ASH ROAD & KELLET. Listening posts out all night. Usual slight retaliation to our mortars in evening by Turn Jars. Draft of 78 to the arrival for Bn.	Fine
	16.			-
	17.		Ordered into Calle Company in morning rest of men accompanied by a few miners. Issues & effects of missing men trench mortar still found theures patrols & 4.5 Howitzer firing during after noon. Advance party of 8th LINCOLN Regt. arrived in forenoon. Day quiet but very wet. Specialists relieved by LINCOLN by Colonel accept Lewis Battalion relief complete 10.a.m. 19th Battalion marched to VERDREL and rest	Wet
	18.			Wet
VERDREL	19		billets then 5 a.m. Total casualties for trench period 7 O Rs wounded (one of which died later). Battalion rested prepared to march on 16 training area next morning.	Fine

T2134. Wt. W708-776. 500000. 4/15. Sir J. C. & S.

WAR DIARY or INTELLIGENCE SUMMARY

Army Form C. 2118.

Place	Date	Hour	Summary of Events and Information	Remarks and references to Appendices
VERDREL	20	8 am	Batln. left VERDREL and marched to MAGNICOURT. 8 miles arriving there 12 midday where they were billeted in MAGNICOURT and HOUVELIN.	
MAGNICOURT	21		No Coln. parade. Inspection and discovery of cases — Bag taken up with made + extemporisation.	
	22		Supervisions made in shot training. Company training carried on in that manner.	
	23		Company training carried on in basis of open warfare.	
	24	9 am	Striking team set aside in case of emergency. Props of Battn. at Baths — Battalion canteens opened.	
	25		Coys & machine platoon (nominal drill carried on.	
	26		Company training. Lectures and albums.	
	27		Company training + range firing by B.A. Coy also Lewis gunners + snipers. training and changes.	
BETHONSART	28		Battn. moved after training to billets in BETHONSART	Montmorency
	29		— do — Tactical exercise in open warfare.	
	30		— do —	
			Royals Northumb (about 10 miles)	

CONFIDENTIAL

Hdqrs Nelson Battn
1. Nov. 1916.

WAR DIARY

of

NELSON BATTALION 189th INFY BGDE

63rd R.N. DIVISION

from

October 1916

to

31 October 1916

To Hdqrs 189th Bde.

E.W. Nelson
Lt Cdr.
Temp. comdg Nelson Bn.
1-11-16

Army Form C. 2118.

WAR DIARY or INTELLIGENCE SUMMARY.
(Erase heading not required.)

_____ Battalion

Hour, Date, Place	Summary of Events and Information	Remarks and references to Appendices
AETHONSART. Oct. 1.	Coy. training. Revd. Revd Ruthie	Dull. Wet.
" 2.	do	
" 3.	Men at training during the day. Preparations for move	
" 4.	Battalion paraded 2.50 am - marched to BELLE EPINE (7½ miles)	Dull
	then to entrained for ACHEUX arriving 6.30 pm - Battalion proceeded	
	by billets and camp on MEPEUX WOOD	
ACHEUX. " 5.	All day taken up cleaning camp, Battalion also bathed - Cinema	Fine
	in evening in Y.M.C.A.	
" 6.	Instruction during day - Concert party Variety report triplung	Showers
" 7.	do	
" 8.	Battalion marched to billets in ENGLE BELMER (The Division has no trams)	
	MAILLET WOOD EAST when it was intended to bivouac to billets was found fully	Heavy showers
	occupied. Working parties of 1 Officer and 50 men and 2 officers & 50	
	men left at VARENNES and MAILLY respectively	
ENGLEBELMER. " 9.	Working parties of offrs & A&Ps do. Make Trench.	Fine
" 10.	do do do. Instruction communication between	Fine
" 11.	Arrived Infantry 13 officers per Coy. 175 men specialists worked the	
	time	
	Brigadier was Battalion out on working parties - including temporary	showers
	parties conty ABS employed A65 dinning dropped to provide back rest in	
" 12.	trenches. Parties of offrs & oors in trenches	
	Coy. training and working parties	
" 13.	" " " " " " L/61 TPs	Dull
	[signature]	

(73989) W.4141—463. 400,000. 9/14. Hj&J Ltd. Forms/C. 2118/10.

Army Form C. 2118.

WAR DIARY
or
INTELLIGENCE SUMMARY.
(Erase heading not required.)

Instructions regarding War Diaries and Intelligence Summaries are contained in F.S. Regs., Part II and the Staff Manual respectively. Title pages will be prepared in manuscript.

Hour, Date, Place		Summary of Events and Information	Remarks and references to Appendices
ENGLEBELMER.	Oct. 15.	Working parties in forenoon only. 200 O.R's. 11 O.R's to Rest Camp AULT.	
	16.	Left ENGLEBELMER to relieve 13th SUSSEX in AUCHONVILLERS Sector. Relief complete 1.30pm. Battalion Regt. Left Centre H.Q. D Redoubt R.B.N. in BOWERY. Enemy artillery active in evening along some frontage & trenches & killing one & wounding another man.	Fair.
AUCHONVILLERS SECTOR	17.	Battalion relieved by ARGYLL & SUTHERLAND HIGHLANDERS. Relief complete 3pm. Battalion returned to billets in ENGLEBELMER.	Fair.
ENGLEBELMER.	18.	Working parties 255 O.R's. Training carried on by Remainder.	Wet.
	19.	—do— 365 —do— Details (party sent out from to TYNHEAD With stacking ammunition dumps (20 O.R's including 10 Bombers)	
	20.	Working party of 100 O.R's. Battalion marched to METAIL (3 miles) taking up positions as follows:— A Coy in dugout line. Hgrs. B.C.D specially in village. Our Artillery active during night.	Fine.
METAIL.	21.	Battalion relieved HAWKE BATT'n in JAMMET Sector. Relief complete 1.30 p.m. M.T. Coys in front line. D in Reserve. Our artillery very active in afternoon from 12 midday. Very slight retaliation. Our working party of 100 men and 4 Officers assisted by covering parties provided with Huggams of New Trenches in front & reached by another route from HOOD and DRAKE Battalions.	Fine.
HAMEL.	22.	Day fairly quiet but a fair day of shelling by our artillery when enemy sending mines - retaliation slight. Same working parties at night.	-

Army Form C. 2118.

WAR DIARY
or
INTELLIGENCE SUMMARY.
(Erase heading not required.)

Instructions regarding War Diaries and Intelligence Summaries are contained in F.S. Regs., Part II. and the Staff Manual respectively. Title pages will be prepared in manuscript.

Hour, Date, Place		Summary of Events and Information	Remarks and references to Appendices
HAMEL.	Oct. 23	Games for yesterday evening. Sent over some tear shells.	
"	" 24	Relief which by MANKS Battalion Relief complete 12.20 am.	
		Coy proceeded independently to Billets in BERTLE BERTMER	
ENGLEBELMER	25	Tricks and Mend. Kit inspection and preparation begun	
		trooops fitting out Billets for Officers.	Sent Appendix I. Order N° 55
	26	" do for Warrants	
	27	Inspection by Brigadier in forenoon –	Very wet. Appendix II Order N° 57.
	28	Parades in fighting order – Co inspection. Working party 200 Oks.	Sick.
	29	Working parties of 100 Oks. Church Parade.	absence
	30	Baleen manches to shelters in VARENNES	
	31	Battalion paraded to am and marched to PUCHEVILLER Going into shelters.	
		there. (6 miles) Transport Bill Stores Afterwards there from MEDAUVILLE	

EStJohn
Lt Col
T Comdg Malson Bttn
7-11-16

confidential

Hqrs Nelson Batt.
1 Dec 1916

Y916

WAR DIARY.

of

NELSON BATTALION 189th INFY. BGDE

63rd R.N. DIVISION.

from

1st November 1916

to

30 November 1916

EW Nelson
Lieut Commr.
Commanding Nelson Batt.
R.N.D.

to Adjt 189 Bde

Army Form C. 2118.

WAR DIARY
or
INTELLIGENCE SUMMARY.
(Erase heading not required.)

Place	Date	Hour	Summary of Events and Information	Remarks and references to Appendices
CHUIGNES	Oct 1		Battalion camp cleaning	
	2		-do- Small working parties on works	
	3		Remainder of Coys bathed. Inspection by G.O.C. 1st Division	
	4		Bn. relieved in line & returned to camp	
	5		Battalion ready march to take van positions by 5th Bde Hd.Qrs.	
	6		Without notice of goto relieve 9th Austr. Battalion marches to ENGLEBELMER warming [?]	
			[illegible] arrived in JEDMINVILLE	
ENGLEBELMER	7		Supplies Officers Mess L returned to ENGLEBELMER	
	8		Battalion took over line of Int. note of [?] — Relief complete 2 p.m. — Day and night patrols active	
AVELUY / Lijperster	9		[illegible]	
			Enemy's artillery active at night — line ordered still — bombarded at 5 pm.	
	10		Relieved [?] 5 Battalion. Relief complete 7 pm. Battalion marches to billets at	
			ENGLEBELMER. Casualties 1 Man killed and 5 O/Rs wounded.	
	11		Battalion resting all injuries	
LA BELMER	12		Y Coy. Battalion moved to MEAULTE A.M — left ARTAIL 5.30 p.m. and arrived at MEAULTE	

WAR DIARY
or
INTELLIGENCE SUMMARY
(Erase heading not required.)

Army Form C. 2118.

[Signature]

Place	Date	Hour	Summary of Events and Information	Remarks and references to Appendices
[Beaumont?]	Nov 13/16		ROBERTS TRENCH. After being shelled with gas shell in addition for 3 days Zero day. Attack took place at 6 am. Artillery barrage opened at equal distances moving to a pace of 100 yards a minute. Hawke Batt. which by prearrangement should have been 150 yards ahead of our front gun aids at Zero. the German barrage was not quite as heavy midway from our front up to went the line our Z were through the original front line. The battalion [?] suffered considerable casualties [?] from a hidden [?] of officers. The first line troops advanced and keeping in touch with the barrage arrived at the deep tracks shortly between the Terraces on 30th line & STATION ROAD known as the TERRACES. After considerable opposition was met with after having been bombed & fought through. Thereupon advanced to Station Road. Bastards then were cleared with little opposition & the advance continued to Green Line without difficulty. Meanwhile the 3rd & 4th waves encountered very heavy machine gun fire and suffered very heavy casualties in reserve. and Lincoln had lost 1st [?] detached ranks ceased to exist as a fighting force. Battalion HQ [moved] [?] Front line at about 1.30 pm and advanced with [?] to [?] [?] but had been [?].	

WAR DIARY or INTELLIGENCE SUMMARY

Army Form C. 2118.

Place	Date	Hour	Summary of Events and Information	Remarks and references to Appendices
	Nov 13th		Very heavy artillery fire from about 5:45 & afterwards transferred that 3 pdr together & the Germans. The 11th Division were still holding on in front of this & thought the Co. and Adjutant were both killed. On being of troops about 100 strong that had got through to the "Green line" continued the advance on the battery lifting and recaptured machine guns in the "Yellow line". Later they went to find that they were not in touch on either flank. After information had been received that troops were holding the yellow line west of BEAUCOURT the battery under orders after took together in the left and in touch with these troops.	
			During this time the battalion claimed to exist as an identity. A considerable number of prisoners took part in the further advance by ourselves of BEAUCOURT.	
			That nothing the remainder to the formation system surrounded in the advance to attack.	
	Nov 14th /16		On the night of the 14th/15th the Battalion was withdrawn to the Auchonvillers front line system and on the 15th Relieved by KNOLE BELMER. Casualties – Officers killed 2/Lt. No burke, Sub Lieuts J.R. Emerson, E.W. Cashmore, A.L. Ball. L.S. Gardner, D. Francis, E.W. Squirt, E. Langstreth, D.R. Gr. Aldridge, G.A. Reddick	

WAR DIARY
or
INTELLIGENCE SUMMARY.
(Erase heading not required.)

Army Form C. 2118.

Place	Date	Hour	Summary of Events and Information	Remarks and references to Appendices
			Officers Wounded. 2/Lt (Qmr) D. GALLOWAY, 2/Lt. B DANGERFIELD (at duty), S. FLOWITT Sub Lieut. F.S. LLOYD, R.K MITCHELL, A.P. MECKLENBURG, J.R. SMYTH, F.W GIARDIN, E.V.G. GARDNER (at duty)	
			Other Ranks :- Killed 34	
			Wounded 195 + 2 at duty	
			Missing 130	
			Gassed 1	
	Nov 15th		Battalion marched to HEDAUVILLE with half at ENGLEBELMER In evening proceeded to ARQUEVES	
	16		by motor lorries (bus) via Acheux team.	
			Remained at ARQUEVES. Reorganising and voting at enrolment/particulars	
	17		same as for 16	
	18		Battalion proceeded by march route to GEZAINCOURT taking up Billets there for the night	
	19		Marched to CANDAS (Am/s) - Billets	
	20		Inspection by General Sweard an Commander in Chief	
AMIENS	21		Battalion marched to DOMQUEUR (11 miles) taking up Billets for the night	
	22		Proceeded by march route to ONEUX - overnight then also	
	23		Marched to GRAND LAVIERS	

WAR DIARY
or
INTELLIGENCE SUMMARY.

Army Form C. 2118.

Place	Date	Hour	Summary of Events and Information	Remarks and references to Appendices
	1917 Jan 24		Relief completed journey to Australian LF CHAMPNEUF going into billets there for reorganization and training	
MAMPNEUF	25		Reorganization of Companies. Recd 14/2 Otto Reinforcements	
	26		Company commenced Company arm drill - trade work - lectures - ½ Otto reinforcements arrived	
	27		Continued training - Company (Companies?) in platoon	
	28		do — Bayonet fighting and skill at arms	
	29		Route march. Command drill. Afternoon all to be worked to game	
	30		Transport and all to completed by Brigadier Bayonet fighting lectures	

E.W. Nelson Lt. Cd.
Commanding Nelson Battn.

SECRET.   APPENDIX I   Spare

NELSON BATTALION ORDER 50   War Diary

October 25th, 1916

Reference Double Strip Map 1/10,000.

1. PLAN (a) The 189th Infantry Brigade will take part in an attack which will be made on the Enemy's position on both sides of the RIVER ANCRE.
(b) The date of the attack will be known as "Z" day, Zero time will be notified later.

2. BRIGADE LIMITS From Railway Road to about Q 17 d 35.79.

3. BRIGADE FORMATION The Brigade will attack with two Battalions in the first line and two Battalions following. HOOD will be on the right and HAWKE on the left.
   DRAKE in rear of HOOD
   NELSON in rear of HAWKE
The 188th Infantry Brigade will be on the left of the 189th Infantry Brigade.

4. PLAN OF ATTACK NELSON will be formed up in four waves immediately in rear of HAWKE under and close up to the Bank behind ROBERTS TRENCH left flank resting on LOUVERCY STREET. Each such wave will consist of four platoons, one from each Company, and will be formed from right to left as follows:-
   A Company, C, D, & B.
Waves will follow each other at distances of ten yards between first and second waves and forty yards between second and third and third and fourth. The leading wave will follow fourth wave of HAWKE at a distance of 150 yards. The initial obstacles in front of the NELSON'S, and not in front of the HAWKE'S, will necessitate the NELSON'S moving off as fast as possible after the HAWKE'S. The distance of 150 yards is to be adjusted after we have passed our front line trench.

5. OBJECTIVE HOOD and HAWKE will capture the <u>first objective</u> i.e. Reserve Trench in Enemy's Front System (<u>Dotted Green Line</u>) and will clean up all three lines. This Objective will be captured at 0 hours 18'.
   SECOND OBJECTIVE at 0 hours 23' DRAKE and NELSON will pass through HOOD and HAWKE and will capture the GREEN LINE. The first and second waves will advance straight through to this line and reorganise at once. The third wave will clear up the dug-outs in STATION ROAD and the fourth wave will clear up the DOTTED BLUE LINE, and the many dug-outs on the reverse slope of the Hill.
   There will be a halt of about 30 minutes on the GREEN LINE, during which there will be two pauses of 5 minutes in the 18 pdrs. barrage.
   At the end of the second pause an intense barrage will reopen and HOOD and HAWKE will pass through DRAKE and NELSON and capture the YELLOW LINE. There will be a halt of about half an hour on the YELLOW LINE, during which time DRAKE and NELSON will close up to within 150 yards of HOOD and HAWKE.
   At 2 hours 15' barrage pauses for 5 minutes, on reopening of intense barrage at 2 hours 20' DRAKE and NELSON will advance against the DOTTED YELLOW LINE, where a halt of five minutes will be made, during which HOOD and HAWKE

will pass through DRAKE and NELSON and will advance on the DOTTED BROWN LINE. Immediately the DOTTED BROWN LINE is captured the whole Brigade less HOOD will advance and consolidate the BLUE LINE. Battle patrols will be sent forward from this line.

6. AEROPLANE CO-OPERATION   Flares will be lit, one per twenty-five yards of front:-
   (a) On obtaining each Objective.
   (b) Whenever hung up.
   (c) When an aeroplane sounds its Klaxon Horn.
   (d) Just before dusk and in the early morning if an aeroplane is above.

7. TANKS   Tanks acting under separate orders will support the troops, who are to be warned not to wait for them.

8. EQUIPMENT   Fighting Order :- Greatcoats will be worn with skirts hooked back - method of same will be indicated to Coys. Equipment worn over Greatcoat; haversacks on back containing one Iron Ration, one ration for "Z" day. Four sandbags (two each side under belt and tied). Two Gas Helmets. W.P. Sheet and Mess Tin on back of belt. One Verry's Light and one Flare in left pocket of Service Dress Jacket. Mill's Grenades at the rate of two per man to be carried in sandbags. As many wire cutters as obtainable.

Men carrying wire cutters are to wear a Yellow armlet.
Runners, lightly equipped,- rifle, bayonet & 50 rds. S.A.A. will wear a Blue armlet with a White stripe.

9. BRIGADE HEADQUARTERS   Advanced Brigade H.Qrts. will be established in CHARLES AVENUE, Q.23.c.2.9. at 4 p.m. on "Y" day.

10. HEADQUARTERS   Battalion H.Qrts. on Y/Z night will be in rear of the Bank behind ROBERTS TRENCH close to LOUVERCY STREET. During the Advance Battalion H.Qrts. will move to successive positions in rear of the Centre of the Battalion and will be marked by a Blue & Yellow Flag (Horizontal).

11. BARRAGE   Tables are issued to all Officers. The whole success of the operations depends on the Infantry keeping close up to the Artillery Barrage.

12. LEWIS GUNS   Two Headquarter Lewis Guns will be attached to B & D Coys. (one each). Company and Attached Headquarter Guns will advance with their Coy., one in first wave and one in third wave. The two remaining Headquarter Guns will be held under Commanding Officer at Battalion H.Qrts.

13. BOMBERS   One double group of Headquarter Bombers will be attached to each Coy. These will be detailed by Bombing Officer and will carry "P" Bombs in addition to Mill's Grenades.

14. GENERAL   It must be impressed on all ranks that they are on no account to halt because Units on either flanks are held up. The best way to assist neighbours on such occasions is to continue to advance.

No papers likely to be of value to the enemy to be taken over the parapet.

Unmarked maps of trenches and barrage tables will be taken.

The very strictest orders are to be issued to the men that they must lie perfectly still when it begins to get light on the morning of "Z" day, as observation will probably result in heavy losses before the attack begins.

Men will be wakened up without noise at 5 a.m.

The success of the whole operation depends on an entire absence of noise and movement after day-break.

Watches will be synchronised at times which will be issued later - this should include all ranks in possession of watches.

The necessity of constantly keeping Battalion Headquarters informed of the position of Companies and other information is again impressed on all Officers and N.C.O.s.

Adjutant,
for O.C. NELSON Battalion.

Copies to:-
1. C.O.
2. O.C. A Coy.
3. O.C. B Coy.
4. O.C. C Coy.
5. O.C. D Coy.
6. L.G.O.
7. Bn.B.O.
8. Sig.Officer
9. O.C. Hood
10. O.C. Hawke
11. O.C. Drake   For information
12. 189th.Inf.Bde.
13. Right Battn. 188 Inf.Bde. (through 189th.Inf.Bde).
14 & 15 File.

TIME TABLE.

To be used in connection with barrage table.

HAWKE						
TIME OF COMPLETE CAPTURE (OR ARRIVAL)	+0.18	+0.50	+1.50	+2.50	+3.25	
TIME OF LEAVING		+1.10	About 2.25, After Nelsons pass.	No pause +2.55		
Barrage	DOTTED BLUE	DOTTED GREEN	GREEN	YELLOW ←150x→	DOTTED YELLOW	DOTTED BROWN	BLUE
NELSON						
TIME OF COMPLETE CAPTURE (OR ARRIVAL)		+0.40	—	+2.34	+2.55	+3.35
TIME OF LEAVING		+1.10 (After Hawke's leave)	+2.20			

Notes (Nelson actions):
- NELSONS pass right through.
- 3rd & 4th waves move up & follow on quickly.
- ½ hour (1st and 2nd) REORGANISE WAVES ETC.
- Lie down in 4 waves behind HAWKES.
- NELSONS pass through HAWKES.
- HAWKES pass through NELSONS.
- No pause.
- DIG IN. CONSOLIDATE. REORGANISE. PUT OUT PATROLS.

Stamp: NELSON B[attalion], 26 OCT 1916, BRIGADE, 18910

APPENDIX II

Nelson Battalion Order No. 51.

October 27th 1916.

Administrative Arrangements.

<u>Casualties</u>. Unit Commanders will render the following Casualty Returns during heavy fighting:- A. "Estimated Casualties". These are not official and are not published. No distinction to be made between Killed, Wounded & missing. To be rendered twice daily. Company Commanders must not look upon this return in the light of a useless return called for at a busy time.

It should be remembered that the prompt reinforcing of the Battalion depends upon it.

B. "Actual Casualties". These are official and published casualties. Care should be taken to be exact. All Officers' casualties will be mentioned by name, and in the event of Unit Commanders, the names of Officers taking over Command. During heavy fighting this return will be rendered so as to reach Headquarters by 2 p.m. and will include casualties for preceding 24 hours, noon to noon.

<u>S.O.S.</u> The Signal Officer will be responsible for always having an S.O.S. signal with him.

<u>Prisoners</u>. All prisoners will first be disarmed and escorted to the rear, where they will be taken over under Brigade arrangements. Not more than 2 men will accompany every 50 prisoners.

Petrol tins. Empty petrol tins must always be returned for full ones. Care should also be taken to return stoppers with the tins.

Field Kitchens. It is hoped that one Field Kitchen per Battalion will be got up as far as Hamel.

Only 5 cooks from the Battalion are required to attend the Kitchens, 2 of whom will be with the forward Kitchen. 'C' Company will detail 2 cooks, A, B, & D one cook each.

Preservation of supplies etc. Attention is again called to the extreme urgency of preserving ammunition and supplies. Flares, torches etc., issued must be kept dry as far as possible, and men should be particularly warned as to the folly and wanton crime of endeavouring to rid themselves of weight by dumping bombs or other material in trenches as they advance.

Nominal Rolls. Nominal Rolls will be prepared by each Company, Signal Officer, Lewis Gun Officer and Headquarters, of all personnel accompanying respective Units.

This must be corrected from day to day as personnel is detached for special work etc.

These returns will be handed in to the Orderly Room and sent to the Battalion base for safe custody.

All specialists ordered in Preliminary Instructions, or subsequent orders, to be attached to Companys, will report today to the respective Coys. and come under Command of those Coys. upon reporting. They will be rationed & billeted by Companies and included in the Nominal Rolls referred to.

Surplus Gear. All surplus gear not accompanying the Battalion will be dumped in an unoccupied billet in ENGLEBELMER at barn adjoining Town Major's Office, Billet No. 104.

Three men's gear will be packed in one sandbag, and all sandbags are to be properly labelled. All Units will make their own arrangements so that this regulation can be carried out at the shortest notice.

Documents. All Official documents, duplicate nominal rolls, conduct sheets &c., will be handed in to Orderly Room for safe custody, securely packed and labelled.

Surplus Officers. Surplus Officers will report to Major Norris on Y day.

Ammunition. Supplies of ammunition &c may be drawn from any dump.

Rations. Rations will only be supplied from 189th Infantry Brigade dump. All rations will be packed in sandbags containing 10 rations each. Rations can be had on the chit of an Officer, who should state the name of the Battalion. Rations will not be demanded from Battalion Headquarters, but direct from the dump.

Carrying parties. Sufficient men to carry the rations or ammunition required will always be sent back with the demand, and, to prevent men being arrested as deserters or stragglers, parties should always be properly conducted, or the men should have written authority to return given them, signed by an Officer.

J H Smerill Sub/Lt
Adjutant
for O.C. Nelson Battalion.

CONFIDENTIAL

Headquarters, NELSON BATTN.

December 31st.1916.

W A R   D I A R Y

OF

N E L S O N   B A T T A L I O N

FROM

D ECEMBER 1st 1916

TO

DECEMBER 31st.1916.

To,
   Headquarters,
      189th.Infantry Brigade.

Lieutenant, R.N.V.R.
Commdg.NELSON Battalion.

Army Form C. 2118.

WAR DIARY
or
INTELLIGENCE SUMMARY.
(Erase heading not required.)

NELSON Batt'n.

Hour, Date, Place		Summary of Events and Information	Remarks and references to Appendices
Dec 1st	Le Champenuf	Platoon Drill, Bayonet fighting, Lectures. 27 OR Reinforcements.	
2nd	do	Armourer inspected barrels of rifles. Inoculation started.	
3rd	do	Roman Catholic Service in St Firmin Ch, other denominations service on Parade ground.	
4th	do	Ceremonial Parade and Arm drill. Firing practice. Bayonet fighting.	
5th	do	Company close order drill and communication drill. 43 OR Reinforcements.	
6th	do	Route march accompanied by Transport.	
7th	do	Arm drill. Musketry. Bayonet fighting.	
8th	do	Bayonet fighting under Army Instructor.	
9th	do	Battalion Drill.	
10th	do	Church Parades as for last week.	
11th	do	Coy and arm drill. Musketry.	
12th	do	Arm drill. Bayonet fighting. Our posts.	
13th	do	do	Military Medal awarded to LS HG. FOX and AB. J McLEOD.
14th	do	Arm drill. Bayonet fighting. Musketry Lecture by MO. 140 OR and Sub Lt CLERK & FAIR joined Battalion.	
15th	do	Wiring exercises. Advancing by waves. Taking up positions in the dark. 11 OR and 16 officers Reinforcements. Lt BUCKLE, Sub Lts WICKS, NOWELL, BRIDGE, BLOOMFIELD, HEWITT, HUNT, BROWN, TAYLOR, WELLWOOD, WOLFE, SIDDLE, HABGOOD, HUCKLEBRIDGE, BOWLER, HOWARD	
16th	do	Arm drill. Battalion drill attack.	
17th	do	Church services as for last week.	

Fred O'Hare
Lt RNVR
Cdg NELSON BATT'N

Army Form C. 2118.

WAR DIARY
or
INTELLIGENCE SUMMARY.
(Erase heading not required.)

NELSON Battn.

Hour, Date, Place	Summary of Events and Information	Remarks and references to Appendices
Dec 18/15 Champneuf	Musketry, Bayonet fighting, Coy drill. Specialists training.	
19/15 do.	Brigade Route march (10 miles) Specialist training in afternoons.	
20/15 do.	Arm drill Bayonet fighting, Coy drill Advances by waves. Reorganising Sub Lt E.V. GARDNER awarded Military Cross	
21st do.	Arm drill Bayonet fighting. Laying out trenches, methods of carrying out reliefs.	
22nd do.	Arm drill. Route march. C Coy digging on Bdy Training Trenches.	
23rd do.	Lt Iles RAMC temp apptM.O vide Surgeon Cox on leave.	
24/15 do.	Arm drill Battalion Outpost Scheme. Specialist training bayonet fighting.	
25/15 do.	Church services as for previous week.	
26/15 do.	Church services as for yesterday. General leave.	
27/15 do.	Ceremonial parade arm drill range bayonet fighting. Visit by G.O.C. Court Martial on Sub Lt Syett at Battalion HQ.	
28/15 do.	Attacking in waves. Bdy Trenches. Court of Enquiry on AB Ball. Lt TURNBULL and 16 OR joined as Reinforcements. Arm drill bayonet fighting, wiring patrols specialists. Lieut Spain assumes temporary command of Battn vide Lt Cdr Nelson on leave.	
29/15 do.	Ceremonial parade, arm drill wiring bayonet fighting, specialists	
30/15 do.	Battn Route March. Lt TURNBULL to duty at reinforcement camp Calais.	
31/15 do.	Services as for previous week.	

Shaw.
Lieut. RNVR.
Cdg NELSON BATTN.

Confidential

WAR DIARY

of

NELSON BATTALION 189th BRIGADE

63rd R.N. Division

from

~~1st December 1916~~

to

~~31st December 1916~~

January 1917

E.W. Nelson
Comdr.
Cdg. Nelson Btn.

Army Form C. 2118.

WAR DIARY
or
INTELLIGENCE SUMMARY.
(Erase heading not required.)

Instructions regarding War Diaries and Intelligence Summaries are contained in F. S. Regs., Part II. and the Staff Manual respectively. Title pages will be prepared in manuscript.

Hour, Date, Place		Summary of Events and Information	Remarks and references to Appendices
1917 January 1	LE CHAMPNEUF	Ceremonial parade and arm drill, Specialists, 1 platoon on Ranges and Company practising attack in woods	
" 2nd	"	Brigade practice attack at VERCOURT.	
" 3rd	"	Battalion practice attack at St FIRMIN.	
" 4th	"	Advanced Guards – Specialists and range	
" 5th	"	Brigade practice attack VERCOURT.	
" 6th	"	Company drill and specialists	
" 7th	"	Church services for fine weather.	
" 8th	"	Company drill – Specialists	
" 9th	"	Battalion practice attack VERCOURT	
" 10th	"	Route March – LA CAISSÉE, LE CROTOY, BECALBARALLES, LE CHAMPNEUF	
" 11th	"	Company drill and practising advancing in waves.	
" 12th	"	Gas lecture & drill, lecture on march discipline and discipline.	
" 13th	"	Battalion proceeded by march route to Billets at DRUCAT (15 miles).	
" 14th	"	Battalion marched to CAPENNES (London) to map at Billets there.	
" 15th	CAPENNES	Battalion continued march to CANDAS going into billets there.	
" 16th	CANDAS	Remained at CANDAS.	
" 17th	"	Marched to RUBEMPRE taking up White Hut (10 miles)	
" 18th	RUBEMPRE	Battalion proceeded by Motor Buses to Lancashire Dump, thence by route march to BEAUCOURT. Left Sub Sector relieving 11th Battalion 3 Battalions E. Yorks, 6th K. Yorks and Lancs, 9th West Riding Regiment. Relief completed 9.0 a.m. (19th).	(over)

(73989) W4141—463. 400,000. 9/14. H.&I. Ltd. Forms/C. 2118/10.

Army Form C. 2118.

WAR DIARY
or
INTELLIGENCE SUMMARY.
(Erase heading not required.)

Instructions regarding War Diaries and Intelligence Summaries are contained in F.S. Regs., Part II. and the Staff Manual respectively. Title pages will be prepared in manuscript.

Hour, Date, Place	Summary of Events and Information	Remarks and references to Appendices
1917		
January 19th BEAUCOURT (LEFT)	Posts pushed out and consolidation of 1st line begun. Enemy artillery very active.	
20th "	Consolidation of front system continued. Enemy hostile of 2 O.R.s. Artillery both sides active.	
21st "	Forward and Sap found. Enemy observed at intervals varying from 200 to 1000 yards. Heavy artillery bombardment continued throughout the day. Considerable retaliation and intermittent shelling from our own batteries.	
22nd "	Consolidation of outposts and front line system continued. Artillery active on both sides. Battalion relieved by HAWKE BATTn. Relief completed by 11.0 pm. Battn took up quarters in Mesnil Junction.	
23–26 BEAUCOURT (SUPPORT)	The whole Battalion engaged on working and carrying parties. Clearing up round the line. No events available.	
27th "	Working and carrying parties as above. 1 Platoon sent off to C.C.S. VARENNES. Battalion relieved by Public Fusilier Regt. completed by 10 pm. Battalion proceeded to FORCEVILLE by route march via LANCASHIRE DUMP, BOUZINCOURT, HEDAUVILLE arriving 12.30 AM 28th in Billets	
28th FORCEVILLE	Battalion engaged in cleaning up — making amends	
29th "	Four Platoons on Working parties. Remainder kitting up.	
30th "	Lectures at Battalion by Company Commanders in forenoon. Box Respirators tested. Divisional Band played.	
31st "	Battalion inspected by Brigadier. All Companies & H.Q. bathed in local baths.	

Confidential.   H.Qs Nelson Bn.

WAR DIARY.
of
NELSON Battn — 189th Bde.
63rd R.N. Dvn.

from.

1st February. 1917.
to.
28th February. 1917.

To/
HQs
189th Bde.

E. Wilson.
Cdr.
Commanding Nelson Bn.

Vol 9

WAR DIARY
INTELLIGENCE SUMMARY.

(Erase heading not required.)

Army Form C. 2118.

Nelson Batt.

Instructions regarding War Diaries and Intelligence Summaries are contained in F.S. Regs., Part II. and the Staff Manual respectively. Title pages will be prepared in manuscript.

Hour, Date, Place		Summary of Events and Information	Remarks and references to Appendices
Feb 1st 1917.	BEAUCOURT.	Battalion paraded at FORCEVILLE at 11am and marched to Frenchies having lunch and tea en route; taking up position in the evening. Relief complete by 10.30pm "D" Coy in front line. "A" in YORKSHIRE TR. "B" in SUVLA TR. and "C" in CAVES. Test F (one round shrapnel) at midnight fired in 3½ mins by Battery B 223 at 11.30pm man killed in post 12, by own shelling, artillery notified shells falling short.	Very cold, frosty and bright weather.
Feb 2nd	do	During the night three Coys engaged in connecting and altering posts in front line and YORKSHIRE TR. Work on new dugout R1 & B 6 commenced. Test Barrage in operation at following times 8.45pm, 9.15pm, 9.45pm. Enemy replied between 9.25 – 9.35pm. Hostile Artillery very active. Casualties: "13" post 1 killed.	do
Feb 3rd	do	Intermittent shelling during the morning on both sides.	For full account of operations Feb 1st – Feb 5th inclusive see Appendices I. II. III. IV. and report on operations before BEAUCOURT.
Feb 4th	do	(For confirmation of operations see attached report.) Relieved in front line Frenchies by 4th BEDFORD Regt during the evening and retired to support line arriving about 10pm.	Very cold, frosty and bright weather.
Feb 5th	do	Day spent in cleaning dug-outs which has been left in a filthy condition. Working party in evening.	do
Feb 6th	do	Working parties whole Battalion.	do
Feb 7th	do	do	do
Feb 8th	do	do	do
Feb 9th	do	do	do

WAR DIARY
or
INTELLIGENCE SUMMARY.

(Erase heading not required.)

Army Form C. 2118.

Instructions regarding War Diaries and Intelligence Summaries are contained in F.S. Regs., Part II and the Staff Manual respectively. Title pages will be prepared in manuscript.

Hour, Date, Place	Summary of Events and Information	Remarks and references to Appendices
Feb. 10th BEAUCOURT. ENGLEBELMER.	Coy. of Engineers or Hawke HQ. ENGLEBELMER as to gap in fighting line between Hawke and Nelson Battalions during operations. Battn. relieved in line by Hawke Bn. and moved into billets in ENGLEBELMER. Two Coys. moved on to LEALVILLERS. The latter being under the direction of the Director of Transportation for work.	Cold frosty bright weather
Feb. 11th ENGLEBELMER. LEALVILLERS.	Continuation of Court of Enquiry held at Nelson HQ. ENGLEBELMER.	do.
Feb. 12th do.	Two Coys. move to support line to act as carrying party to 190 Bde. Conclusion of Court of Enquiry held at Hawke HQ in support line.	Thaw set in
Feb. 13th THIEPVAL. FORCEVILLE ENGLEBELMER. LEALVILLERS.	Two Coys. move to THIEPVAL for work under C.R.E. Battn. HQ. move to FORCEVILLE. Two Coys at LEALVILLERS.	do.
Feb. 14th do	Coys. as working parties in respective areas	do.
Feb. 15th do	do.	do.
Feb. 16th do (front line system)	Two Coys. move to old German front line system on NORTH side of ANCRE. for carrying work.	Fine.
Feb. 17th do	do.	do.

WAR DIARY or **INTELLIGENCE SUMMARY.**
(Erase heading not required.)

Army Form C. 2118.

Instructions regarding War Diaries and Intelligence Summaries are contained in F.S. Regs., Part II. and the Staff Manual respectively. Title pages will be prepared in manuscript.

Hour, Date, Place		Summary of Events and Information	Remarks and references to Appendices
Feb 18th	THIEPVAL FORCEVILLE LEALVILLERS	Two Coys move back to THIEPVAL.	Thirsty
Feb 19th	HEDAUVILLE	Battln. HQ move to HEDAUVILLE. Coys as working parties in respective areas.	do.
Feb 20th	do	do	do.
Feb 21st	do.	do	Fine
Feb 22nd	do.	Coys at LEALVILLERS interchange with those at THIERVAL, the Coys at THIEPVAL moving to VARENNES.	do
Feb 23rd	do.	Coys. working in respective areas.	do
Feb 24th	do	Coys working in respective areas.	Thirsty
Feb 25th	THIEPVAL HEDAUVILLE VARENNES.	do.	Thirsty
Feb 26th	do.	Bn. HQ and two Coys VARENNES move to Spring Garden Camp POZ. Two Tents erected so sleep in Gum Boot Store.	Thirsty
Feb 27th	THIEPVAL POZ	Two Coys POZ work for Australian Troops. Tents erected and coys and HQ move in. Coys THIEPVAL working parties.	Thirsty
Feb 28th	POZ	Improvement to camp. Two coys working for Australian troops. Two Coys THIEPVAL move into camp.	Thirsty

E. Snelson Comdg.
1-3-19

NELSON BATTALION, 63RD., (R.N.) DIVISION.

REPORT ON OPERATIONS BEFORE BEAUCOURT DURING PERIOD FEBRUARY 1ST.,
TO FEBRUARY 5TH., INCLUSIVE.

February 1st.   The NELSON Battalion relieved the left sub-section of the left Brigade area on the night of February 1st./ 2nd., taking up the following dispositions:-

No. 1 Company :- Line of posts and partially dug trench from No. 10 post, right limit of Battalion sub-section, to No. 15 post, left limit of Brigade sector. This line is known in this report as OUTPOST line. Also line of forward posts lettered from "A" to "E" in front of OUTPOST line, known as lettered posts.

No. 2 Company :- YORKSHIRE TRENCH.

No. 3 Company :- HOSPITAL DUG-OUTS at R.7.b.47 with battle position in SUVLA TRENCH and finding 4 posts in SUVLA as right platoon markers for battle position.

No. 4 Company :- The CAVES at R.7.c.78 in reserve.

February 2nd.   On the nights of February 1st., and 2nd., small alterations in location of posts were made, so that forward positions on February 3rd., were as follows :-

Post.	Co-ordinates.	Remarks.
A	R.2.a.25.	
B.	R.2.a.05.	
B₂.	R.1.b.74.	A new post.
C.	R.1.b.34.	Moved forward 100 yards.
D.	R.1.b.03.	Moved forward 75 yards and 20 yards to left on to top of bank. A very fine commanding position.
E.	R.1.a.62.	
10.	R.2.a.00.	
11.	R.1.b.91.	
12.	R.1.b.82.	
13.	R.1.b.62.	
13a.	R.1.b.43.	A new post.
14.	R.1.b.11.	
15.	R.1.a.71.	

February 3rd.   At dusk on February 3rd., the following dispositions were made without incident :-

No. 1 Company :- Posts A, B, B₂
ARTILLERY ALLEY from A to Post 11.
Posts 11, 12.
No. 1 Company kept 1 platoon in readiness to advance up

February 3rd.   No. 2 Company :- Posts C, D, E.
                                  Posts 13, 13a, 14, 15.

               No. 3 Company :- Right of YORKSHIRE TRENCH.

               No. 4 Company :- A series of partially dug trenches known as the SHELL SLITS, to the immediate right of PUSIEUX ROAD in continuation of YORKSHIRE TRENCH southwards.

Zero was fixed for 11 p.m. February 3rd.

At 10.50 p.m., Nos. 3 and 4 Companies moved up in Artillery formation to behind No. 2 and No. 1 Battalion respectively, taking up positions in the OUTPOST line on vacation of same by supporting Companies of Nos. 2 and 1 Battalions.

One Company of No. 4 Battalion was placed at the disposal of the C.O., and placed in YORKSHIRE TRENCH.
The intention was that Nos. 1 and 2 Battalions should assault and capture PUSIEUX and RIVER TRENCHES and that No. 3 Battalion should form a defensive flank from R.2.a.46 to ~~right~~ of Brigade sector, No. 4 Battalion remaining in reserve.

At Zero our barrage opened and Nos. 1 and 2 Battalions advanced to the attack.

The platoon of No. 1 Company detailed for post at R.2.a.46 advanced behind the last wave of No. 2 Battalion and took up a position judged to be correct.

Meanwhile a platoon of No. 2 Battalion took up a position between Posts A and B and commenced digging in. The Officer in charge was convinced that this was his correct position. No instructions had been given to Headquarters, No. 3 Battalion regarding this.

February 4th.   By programme the left of No. 2 Battalion should have rested on our post at R.2.a.46 but touch could not be established. A patrol was therefore sent out along ARTILLERY ALLEY at 12.30 a.m., to clear the situation. This patrol after two hours absence sent back a report to the effect that the patrol was held up a few yards from an enemy post. Further reconnaisance revealed that this post was situated about R.2.a.68 to R.2.a.65.
A bombing patrol was sent out but failed to dislodge the enemy and reported that the post was effectively wired. The enemy post had a very good field of fire and was keeping up a considerable volume of rifle fire.

Since the reduction of this post threatened to involve a considerable number of men, and having regard to the absence of immediate support for defensive purposes, the O.C., No. 1 Company did not feel justified in taking more extensive action without reference to Headquarters.

No anxiety had been felt at Headquarters about the right flank because a message had been received at 2.10 a.m. from the Report Centre to the effect that No. 1 Company was in touch with No. 2 Battalion. At 7.30 a.m., when information was received that there was a gap in the line in ARTILLERY ALLEY

February 4th. to keep this gap under close observation and attack immediately in a north easterly direction should enemy appear.

During this period the enemy artillery showed no unusual activity. In answer to our barrage the enemy opened light barrage fire on our front system and area about SUVLA.
The only position where enemy fire was from time to time intense was PUSIEUX ROAD, which position was kept under heavy fire from 4.2 and 5.9 howitzers.

At 10 a.m., orders were received to send the Company of No. 4 Battalion in YORKSHIRE TRENCH to Re-enforce No. 1 Battalion. Orders as requisite and report received that Company had moved off at 10.30 a.m. O.C., No. 1 Battalion informed.
At 11.30 a.m., verbal orders were received from the G.O.C, 189th., Brigade, to assault and occupy the post held by the enemy in ARTILLERY ALLEY, and to detail No. 3 Company to assault and occupy a strong point still held by the enemy in PUSIEUX TRENCH. These orders were transmitted to those concerned immediately.

Copy.

O.C., No. 1 Company.

Aeroplane photo shows that you did not move far enough up ARTILLERY ALLEY last night.
I have just received your plan of attack. X
Following modifications must be made ÷

You must attack at once in force and take this post at all costs, and report immediately you have occupied it.
Stokes can put up barrage for you.
No. 3 Company will not be available since they are to take another point immediately you have taken this post.

4/2/17. 11.30 a.m. O.C.

X Appendix II.

Copy.

O.C., No. 3 Company.

By arrangement with O.C., No. 2 Battalion, you will attack and occupy the strong point still held by enemy in PUSIEUX TRENCH.
This point will be reduced at all costs.
O.C., No. 1 Company is attacking post at R.2.a.46 at once without assistance from you. It is suggested that your attack should be launched immediately after this post has been taken.

4/2/17. 11.30 a.m. O.C.

(4)

February 4th.   Copy.

O.C., No. 2 Battalion.

By orders of G.O.C., my No. 3 Company will be at your disposal with orders to take the enemy strong point in PUSIEUX TRENCH at all cost.

My No. 1 Company is assaulting enemy post at R.2.a.u.t at once.

G.O.C. suggested that your attack with my No. 3 Company should be launched immediately after my No. 1 Company has occupied the post in ARTILLERY ALLEY.

4/2/17.   11.30 a.m.   O.C.

At 12.30 p.m., the following modification was notified from Brigade :-

"No. 3 Company will not make above attack but remain in close support to No. 1 Company."

Copy.

O.C., No. 3 Company.

Reference my message of the 4th., 11.30 a.m. Cancel these orders.

You will hold the OUTPOST Line from Post 11 at ARTILLERY ALLEY towards the South, remaining in close support to our right northern flank.

You will not be at disposal of O.C., No. 2 Battalion but under my orders.

You will keep in close support to him in every way.   Please inform O.C., No. 2 Battalion and O.C., No. 1 Company.

4/2/17.   12.30 p.m.   O.C.

Copy.

O.C., No. 1 Company.

No. 3 Company is again at our disposal in close support to you.

Arrange with him for what support you need.

Gniping post must be taken at once and at any cost.

Bombs can be obtained from Advanced Brigade Dump at R.1.d.86.

4/2/17.   12.40 p.m.   O.C.

At 5.30 a.m., the 2nd. in Command was personally told by O.C. No. 2 Battalion that one of our Companys in support to the attack (Nos. 3 & 4 Coys.) had been moved up and was holding a position between Nos. 1 and 2 Battalions in the front line.   This information was reported to Brigade Headquarters.

As it was known that No. 3 Company had not moved, it was presumed that No. 4 Company had moved up.   A runner was sent to O.C., No. 1 Battalion at 10.30 a.m., asking for information.   The answer was received at noon, but No 3 Company was not mentioned.   Situation was forwarded to Brigade Headquarters.

February 4th.   At 2.40 p.m., orders were received to send an officers
patrol out to locate No. 4 Company which was immediately
done.
At 3.30 p.m., the C.O., received orders to hand over to
2nd. in Command and report to Brigade Headquarters.
The C.O., returned and resumed command at 4.45 p.m.,
receiving a report from O.C., No. 4 Company to the effect
that he was in position in HOSPITAL Dug-outs, and was moving
into battle position in the SHELL SLITS at dusk.

O.C., No. 4 Company had mis-read his orders (vide Appendix
1, para. 8) and had moved back at dawn into HOSPITAL Dug-outs
without having been relieved.
Headquarters was aware that No. 4 Company had not been
relieved and therefore this position for No. 4 Company was
never considered. . Runners had been passing the entrance
at frequent intervals, but this location was never suspected
and no reports had been received.

At 5.15 p.m., a report was received that the enemy position
in ARTILLERY ALLEY had been captured and was occupied.
The attack was slightly delayed by an enemy aeroplane flying
over ARTILLERY ALLEY, hindering the forming up since it was
feared it might be observed.
The attack was carried out as follows :-

At Zero 5.15 p.m., a Stokes gun situated at R.2.a.3035,
opened 30 rounds barrage fire. On the 20th., round being
fired, the signal was given and the attack launched.
The first two waves of 1 officer and 55 men rushed out and
extended to the left from R.2.1.35. The third wave,
consisting of 1 officer and 15 men found by ~~the~~
No. 2 Battalion from platoon in position between Posts A and
B, advanced direct from that position. O.C., No. 1 Company
advanced with 3rd. wave. A Lewis gun was placed at
R.2.a.35 to give supporting fire.
The position was carried without difficulty.

Sniping and Machine gun fire from the left flank caused most
of our casualties, which total 15 in No. 3 Battalion;
those in No. 2 Battalion are not to hand. Sub. Lieutenant
Wolfe of No. 1 Company was unfortunately hit and has not
since been found.

Rapid fire was opened on the retreating enemy and a number
were brought down.
One prisoner was taken belonging to the 230th. R.I.R.. 1st.,
Battalion, 9th. Kom.

The ground was cleared up to a point 150 yards East of point
R.2.a.68. Men were then withdrawn and the enemy post
consolidated. This post consisted of part of
ARTILLERY ALLEY and the ground adjoining with small sniping
posts dug in and well wired.

An advanced post with a Lewis gun was established at point
R.2.a.68

A patrol was sent out and established touch with No. 2
Battalion at a point 100 yards East of R.2.a.68.

(6)

February 4th. These forward posts were favourably situated for sniping, and by this means and by Lewis gun fire a number of the enemy were hit.

At dusk a report was received from the Brigade O.P. at R.1.b.02, that the enemy had been observed to be advancing from behind PUSIEUX ALLEY at 5.30 p.m. with their right resting on PUSIEUX ROAD, and their left disappearing over the crest of the ridge to the East. They were in two waves and disappeared into PUSIEUX ALLEY. The enemy reappeared in a single wave, estimated 70 strong as far as could be seen, and were engaged by our Artillery, the F.O.O. being situated in this O.P. This advance was also observed from Post D, and 7 magazines were fired in rapid succession at a range of 1200 yards. The observed effect on the enemy was considerable and advance was checked and enemy dispersed.

At 6 p.m. orders were received to move no.4 Company into YORKSHIRE TRENCH. A Company of No. 4 Battalion had been occupying this position without reporting to Battalion Headquarters.

At 7.15 p.m. orders were received to send this Company to report to O.C., No. 1 Battalion. Requisite orders duly issued.

During these operations 4 Lewis guns had been put out of action by hostile gun fire. The Brigade was therefore requested to send up guns to replace these from the reserves. Meanwhile all guns were pushed up from Nos. 3 and 4 Coys, to the front line.

Warning had been received from II Corps that a fresh enemy Regiment had been moved up into the Battle area. This, coupled with the advance observed at dusk, strongly supported the expectation of counter-attack that night. All ranks eagerly awaited same.

At about 9 p.m., the enemy opened an intense barrage along the Northern front, with a secondary barrage chiefly of 5.9 and 4.2 howitzer shells on PUSIEUX ROAD and region about SUVLA and Divisional Track.
The F.O.O. opened 2 rounds gun fire per minute on S.O.S. lines, increasing by increments of 2 rounds to 8 rounds per minute.
The S.O.S. signal was not sent by the Infantry as no hostile Infantry attack was observed.

The barrage slackened after ½ hour without an Infantry attack developing.
The S.O.S. was observed on the right flank and artillery on both sides was observed to be very active in this region.

At about 11 p.m. 4 Lewis guns from the Brigade in Reserve reported to Headquarters. These were sent forward with 3 guides but only one gun managed to proceed to the front line. The other three lost touch and rejoined their own Battalion in SUVLA right.

February 5th. Flares were distributed along the front line system in expectation of the appearance of a contact aeroplane at dawn. No aeroplane appeared until about noon when flares were lit along the front.

February 5th.   Artillery activity was very much below normal during this day.
No. 3 Battalion was relieved during the evening by the 4th., Bedfordshire Regiment with great ease.
The following arrangements were made :-

Relief for No. 1 Coy. to arrive at R.1.d.69 at 6.30 p.m.
 "   " No. 2 Coy.   "   "   "   "   " 7.30p.m.
 "   " No. 4 Coy.   "   " Headquarters, YORKSHIRE
                                TRENCH at 8 p.m.
No. 3 Company could not be specially relieved since this Company was mixed up with No. 1 Company and relieving Battalion was altering its dispositions.

The arrangements for the supply of rations by Brigade was a very great convenience.   In this connection it is suggested that onions should not be included in bagged off rations, since the tea and sugar were very strongly flavoured.
Tommies Cookers are considered essential since the carrying of hot food, which was successfully performed, draws men from the line for too long a period.

White overalls would be a great benefit to patrols and scouts while snow is on the ground.

A small portable rocket for use in posts would be a great improvement on the very large variety now supplied.
The signal could be repeated from back stations with longer range rockets.

                                        E.W.Nelson.

                                  Commander, R.N.V.R.
                                  Commanding NELSON Battalion.

APPENDIX B.

OPERATION ORDER NO. 7
by
COMMANDER E.W. NELSON, RNVR.,   COMMANDING NELSON BATTALION.

February 2nd. 1917.

1. The 189th., Infantry Brigade will attack PUSIEUX and RIVER trenches from the RIVER ANCRE to where ARTILLERY ALLEY runs into these trenches.

2. Time and date will be notified later.

3. The final objective will be the dug-outs in R.8.b. RIVER TRENCH and thence along the ridge in front of ARTILLERY ALLEY.

4. HOOD (No.1) Battalion will attack on the right, HAWKE (No.2) Battalion on the left, each with one Company in close support. NELSON (No.3) Battalion will be in support and DRAKE (No.4) Battalion in reserve.

5. The front will be divided between attacking Battalions by a line drawn through R.2.d.85.

6. At Zero Barrage will open on PUSIEUX TRENCH and 50 yards in front.

Zero + 1 :- Barrage concentrates on PUSIEUX TRENCH.
Zero + 6 :- Barrage lifts to RIVER TRENCH.
Zero + 8 :- Barrage lifts by 100 yards every 4 minutes to line of BAILLESCOURT FARM - PUSIEUX ROAD.
Zero + 60 :- Barrage ceases.

7. A false barrage will be formed on the left flank of the attack.

8. At dusk Companies will move and take up the following positions :-

"D" Company will take up and consolidate a line from R.2a.46 through R.1.b.34 to present position of Post "B". "D" Company will also hold posts 14 and 15.

"B" Company will take up and consolidate a line from R.2a.46 on the right along ARTILLERY ALLEY to Post 11, thence through Posts 12 and 13 to PUSIEUX ROAD.

"A" Company will close up into the Eastern end of YORKSHIRE and the new portions of trench dug along Eastern bank of PUSIEUX ROAD (known as SHELL SLITS) and start improving and extending this line.

"C" Company will move into HOSPITAL Dug-outs and furnish carrying parties requisite.

"D" and "B" Companies will hold the line as above at all costs until relieved on, possibly February 5th., 1917. Listening Posts must be pushed out during the night.

At, or about Zero, "C" and "A" Companies will move in Artillery formation and take up positions on the Outpost line running between BOIS D'HOLLANDE and No. 10 Post.

CONTINUED.

"C" Company will be on the right behind the HOOD Battalion and "A" Company on the left behind the HAWKE Battalion. O's C. "A" and "C" Companies will use their discretion according to light conditions, hostile activity etc., as to exact time they will move into Outpost Line. They will hold this line until relieved at dawn next day, or until relieved later, when "A" Company will move back into YORKSHIRE TRENCH, and "C" Company in HOSPITAL Dug-outs, with Battle position in Shell slits.

Battle positions will be occupied from "stand to" until "stand to", until Battalion is relieved. Dug-outs are not to be occupied during the night.

9. One Company of the DRAKE Battalion has been placed at disposal of O.C. This Company will take up a position in SUVLA until "A" Company has moved out of YORKSHIRE TRENCH, when DRAKE Company will move up into YORKSHIRE TRENCH. O.C. "A" Company will detail guides and make all arrangements with O.C. DRAKE Company.

10. Company Headquarters will be in their respective lines during the nights; during day :-

"D" and "B" at R.1.d.86.
"A" Company in SUVLA.
"C" Company in HOSPITAL Dug-outs.
Battalion Headquarters will not move.

11. Immediately Battle positions have been taken up two runners will be sent to report situation to Battalion Headquarters.

12. Any important information will be first sent to Report Centre at R.1.d.0015, and runners will then come on to Battalion Headquarters with duplicate. Every effort must be made to send information even if purely negative. Report Centre is "C" Company's old Headquarters.

13. Each platoon of "D" and "B" Companies will be provided with the S.O.S. signal, which is WHITE - RED - WHITE. By signal S.O.S. North. This will only be used in the event of attack by Infantry in force.

14. Both next days rations and Emergency days ration will be carried by the men. Water bottles must be filled. Rations will be carried by Brigade arrangements and dumped at R.1.d.86 on nights after operation.

15. Advanced Brigade Dump at R.1.d.86 will supply S.A.A., Water, Wire and all other stores likely to be required.

16. No unwounded man may leave his post to tend wounded. Any man found with any trophy will be tried by F.G.C.M.

17. Prisoners will be sent to HOSPITAL Dug-outs under 5% escorts.

18. Sick Bay will be at the CAVES.

19. Watches will be sent to Battalion Headquarters for synchronisation at 7 p.m. Zero day.

CONTINUED.

20. Copies of these orders must be returned to Battalion Headquarters before Zero. No documents of any possible use to the Enemy will be carried.

21. Men must be warned that the Emergency ration is not an extra ration but will be consumed as requisite and count as that days ration.

                                                      E.W. Nelson

                                                     Commander, RNVR.,
                                      Commanding NELSON Battalion.

Copy.   APPENDIX 2.

O.C., No. 2 Battalion.

                Approximate position of sniping post is R.2.a.4360.

        Proposed plan of attack.
        Time :- 8 p.m.
        Strength :- 1 officer, 40 N.C.O's and men.

                The assaulting party will creep up to within 50 yards and then rush in two waves.

50 men of No. 3 Company will be in support.
The assaulting party will form up at R.2.a.15.

A Lewis gun from No. 3 Company will support and the gun in No. 11 post will move up to R.2.a.2555.

Stokes will fire 6 rounds rapid at Zero.

Will send plan of attack to O.C., No. 2 Battalion and O.C., No. 3 Company who will be required to bring up a supply of Mill's Grenades and "P" bombs.

                If I do not hear I shall assume this course of action is approved.

                I have a post established within 50 yards of the enemy post.

                                      O.C. No. 1 Company.

APPENDIX 3.

DEFENCE SCHEME.

LIMITS :-

    Right limit of sector, a line drawn through :-

        R.2.a.46
        R.7.b.47.
        R.7.c.78.

    Left limit of sector, a line drawn through :-

        R.1.c.72.
        R.7.a.12.

DISPOSITIONS :-

    No. 1 Company:-
        R.2.a.46. A_2
        R.2.a.05.   B.
        R.1.b.74. B_2

        ARTILLERY ALLEY from R.2.a.46 to R.1.b.9510.

        R.1.b.82.   12.
        R.2.a.35.   A.

    No. 2 Company:-
        R.1.b.34.   C.
        R.1.b.03.   D.
        R.1.a.68.   E.
        R.1.b.62.   13.
        R.1.b.43.   13a.
        R.1.b.11.   14.
        R.1.a.71.   15.

    No. 3 Company:-
        R.2.c.19.   9.
        R.2.a.00.   10.
        and shell holes about this region, this Company being in close support to No. 1 Company.

    No. 4 Company:-
        YORKSHIRE TRENCH.

Battalion
H'Quarters:- R.7.a.23.

Sick Bay :- R.7.b.47.

S.O.S.   White - Red - white.

APPENDIX 3. Continued.

ACTION IN CASE OF ATTACK :-

All posts and trenches will be held at all cost.

Should enemy take any post the two posts to its immediate rear will instantly counter-attack without further orders, from half right and half left rear.

Should lodgement of enemy be too extensive for treatment thus, the supporting Companies will counter-attack under their own Commanders.

5/2/17.

E.W. NELSON.
Commander.
Commanding Nelson Battalion.

APPENDIX 4.

Report on Lewis Guns damaged during operations.

1. Completely destroyed.

2.)
) Repairable.
3.)

4. Repaired by Battalion Artificers.

E W Nelson

Commander, R.N.V.R.
Commanding NELSON Battalion.

Appendix V

Casualties:—

Killed 13
Missing 4
Wounded 39

Total 56

EWN

CONFIDENTIAL

Vol 10

WAR DIARY

OF

NELSON BATTALION, 189th. INFANTRY BRIGADE

63rd. (ROYAL NAVAL) DIVISION

FROM

1st. MARCH 1917

TO

31st. MARCH 1917

E W Nelson

Commander, R.N.V.R.
Commanding NELSON Battalion.

Army Form C. 2118.

Nelson Bn

WAR DIARY
or
INTELLIGENCE SUMMARY.
(Erase heading not required.)

Instructions regarding War Diaries and Intelligence Summaries are contained in F.S. Regs., Part II. and the Staff Manual respectively. Title pages will be prepared in manuscript.

Hour, Date, Place		Summary of Events and Information	Remarks and references to Appendices
Spring Garden Camp	Mar. 1st.	Battalion working parties, Courcelette, Miramont Rd. & camp improvements.	
	2.	Do.	
	3.	Do.	
	4.	Church Services	
	5.	Do.	
	6.	Do.	
	7.	Do.	
	8.	Do.	
	9.	Do.	
	10.	Do.	
	11.	Church Services.	
	12.	Do.	
	13.	Do.	
	14.	Do.	
	15.	No working parties. Battalion at Baths.	
	16.	Battalion working parties, Courcelette, Miramont Rd. & camp improvements.	
	17.	Do.	
	18.	Day spent preparing to move. Church Services.	
On the March	19.	Battalion proceeded by Route March to WARLOY. Billets. 9 miles.	
	20.	" " " to billets in PUCHEVILLERS. 6½ miles.	
	21.	" " " " " NEUVILLETTE 12 miles.	
	22.	H.Q. A. & D Coy.s " " " SERICOURT	
		B. & D. Coys. " " " HONVAL	
	23.	Resting. Companies at disposal of Coy. Commanders for cleaning up and feet inspection.	
	24.	Battalion proceeded to billets in VALHUON 11.8 miles.	
	25.	" " " WESTREHEM 9.5 "	
	26.	" " " ANNEZIN 14 "	
ANNEZIN	27.	Companies at disposal of Coy. Commanders. Special attention to be given to deficiencies of kit etc.	

Army Form C. 2118.

Nelson Bn.

WAR DIARY
or
INTELLIGENCE SUMMARY.
(Erase heading not required.)

Instructions regarding War Diaries and Intelligence Summaries are contained in F.S. Regs., Part II. and the Staff Manual respectively. Title pages will be prepared in manuscript.

Place	Date	Hour	Summary of Events and Information	Remarks and references to Appendices
ANNEZIN	Mar. 28.		Bayoney Fighting, Arm Drill, Specialists Training, Lectures.	
	29.		Close order drill, Physical training instruction, Bayonet Fighting, Specialist training.	
	30.		Close order drill & preliminary control by signal. Rapid loading.	
	31.		Bayonet Fighting, Close order drill, Arm drill, Principles of extended order and control by signals, Sentry Groups.	

CONFIDENTIAL

189/63

WAR DIARY

of

NELSON BATTALION. 189 INFANTRY BRIGADE

63rd (ROYAL NAVAL) DIVISION

from

1st April 1917

to

30 April 1917

H.W. Barker Major
for Lt. Colonel
Commanding Nelson Battalion

1st May 1917.

Army Form C. 2118.

WAR DIARY
or
INTELLIGENCE SUMMARY.
(Erase heading not required.)

Instructions regarding War Diaries and Intelligence Summaries are contained in F.S. Regs., Part II. and the Staff Manual respectively. Title pages will be prepared in manuscript.

Place	Date	Hour	Summary of Events and Information	Remarks and references to Appendices
NNEZIN	APRIL 1st		Church Service. Kit inspection by Coy Comdrs. 6.0. inspection of billets	
	2nd		One Platoon per Coy find out ranges.	
	3rd	9.00	Bayonet fighting. P.2. Musketry. Aim Drill. Extending. Rapid Loading. Also of Mills Grenade. Sentry Grps	
		3.00	do	CD + HO Coys (2nd Lt 38 men)
	4th		Failed. 400 Examination by Senior Gas Officer.	
	5th		Training as usual	
	6th		Coys at disposal of OC Coys. Attention to be paid to deployment and formation of wave. Range practice in pm	
	7th		Church service. B Coy baths. Coys at disposal of Coy Commdrs	
	8th		Parade in column of 3's. Training contd'd in pm	
RUITZ	9th	9.30am	Baths. Parade 9.30am and move to RUITZ arriving RUITZ 12 noon. Inds not less than billets until 5pm. All rest and transport cut down to minimum	
	10th		Coys train under own arrangements. Approached Staff standing by at 2 hours notice.	
	11th		Parade at 11am and march to VILLERS BRULIN. 20m to 4pm Lecture by BO on Mills Grenades	
VILLERS BRULIN	12th		Remained at VILLERS BRULIN. Drill at Piquets notice. No training on consequences of bad weather	
ECOIVRES	13th		Passed starting point at BETHUNE START at 11am arrived at X Huts near ECOIVRES at 3pm.	
	14th	2.15pm	Left X Huts ECOIVRES at 2.15pm arriving at Bridge over railway S of Bois de la Haye Blangy at 3pm. Coy Commdrs then reconn. line followed by companies at 7.30pm. Relief completed at 11pm.	
	15th		Left 2 Lieut D.S.O. MoR Ors Commd of Bn from new line commanded EN WILSON BLUR.	
			During the forenoon Brigade on our left advanced towards OPPY-GAVRELLE line. Our forward Coy A was attacked by Platoons from the left about noon an attacking force of DUBLINS and BEDFORDS advanced from our left and changing direction right moved to attack GAVRELLE but on this junction was held up by machine guns and from [?] really shells together with all our lines in rear. During the afternoon an enemy slow shelling was received. Killed 2. Wounded 3. The attacking force of DUBLINS and BEDFORDS with alter or included during the afternoon	
	16th		Enemy artillery markedly active from noon to 3pm. Coy bombers did GAVRELLE and they turned enemy filling own and considerable from our own. At 12EL MADOURI. At 4pm our of Oar Rose was brought down field and	

A5834 Wt W1973/N687 750,000 8/16 D.D. & L. Ltd. Forms/C2118/13.

WAR DIARY
or
INTELLIGENCE SUMMARY

(Erase heading not required.)

Army Form C. 2118.

Place	Date	Hour	Summary of Events and Information	Remarks and references to Appendices
	APRIL 17th		About 1 am "B", "D" Coys who had taken up battle positions on forward MEIN ROAD (near?) GRANGE on left line (ORPY-GAVRELLE) with intention of reoccupying came together with the village of BAILLE B the leading Coy led direction and in consequence of Dly Orders formed up with Points ahead to find travel was heavily mined and much both before WILLERVAL to their original lines behind W.M Boro Sidos Travers Ravine. Willerval and the Railway. Wounded to key sunken road W.M Boro Sidos Travers Ravine.	
	18th		Coys resting and cleaning up. Working Party of 1 Officer and 30 men supplied for carrying party from R.E. dump Pont du Jour to Windsor Rd. Working party supplied.	
	19th		1 NCO and 12 men to work at Rondary. 1 Officer, 182 Platoon to TM School. 1 MO + 40 men to 2nd Field Coy RE.	
	20th 21st		Remainder resting. Area reconnoitred for route to forming up positions. All troops working in circle on important BAILLEUL RR. three Battle Pads and allowed HAMMES BTN Heavily shelled with gas shells on journey where troops carrying annual casualties.	
	22nd		Heavy bombardment during the early morning and forenoon. Several casualties. Our heavy bombarded opp. GAVRELLE line and GAVRELLE village. At 10.30 pm our troops commenced to take up battle positions for assault. Our attack on GAVRELLE	
	23rd		GAVRELLE assaulted by us at 4.45 am an four assaulting good progress was made early and no sign of prisoners taken leading troops were held up by machine gun fire and sniper within village but eventually reached the Yellow line. WIGAN Coy pushing in further advance to the Eastern edge of village drove in masses to reach the BLUE line. By steady and in consequence of activities of MG's and snipers on this GAVRELLE line the enemy had a line shelling the Eastern edge of the village 10 pm from RR with the WINDSOR ST. At about a SINWOOD of this line and trap made by Retain, working from the Margin drawn north to ORPY RR and the RD.	
			(?) Majors Travers South of the Cemetery.	G1923

A8534   Wt. W4973/M687   750,000   8/16   D. D. & L. Ltd.   Forms/C.2113/13.

Army Form C. 2118.

WAR DIARY
or
INTELLIGENCE SUMMARY.
(Erase heading not required.)

Instructions regarding War Diaries and Intelligence Summaries are contained in F. S. Regs., Part II. and the Staff Manual respectively. Title pages will be prepared in manuscript.

Place	Date	Hour	Summary of Events and Information	Remarks and references to Appendices
	April 24th		Enemy furiously bombarded GAVRELLE from 10.3 am to 12 noon during which time he massed for attack and from 3.30 pm onwards kept up heavy artillery on line in front. At no point did he gain any success and suffered severely. We held our line. Old mid throughout the night.	
	25th		Battn kept down in reserve relieved by the Howe Bn and returned by platoons to old trenches St LAURENT BLANCY proceeding by mules thence to MARCEUIL to billets.	
ARCEUIL	26th		Inspection of kit and general reorganization of companies.	
	27th		Running and making parade by 2 have been breakfast. Mattins as a day parade. Battalion was for	
			several Baths and all after were inspected by Armourer. Working parties to scrounging took under TOWN MAJOR	
VILLERS BRUIN	28th		March to VILLERS BRUIN arriving midday about 12.p.m.	
	29th		Battalion preceded by Band march to billets at BEUGIN	
BEUGIN	30		Training commenced - Battalion marched out to training ground at 9 am returning to Camp at 4.30 pm.	Frank Sargisson Lieut & Adjutant

Vol 12

Miss Drury
by
Nelson Bell – 129 Bdy
6.3 m R.N Division
from
1st April 1917
*
31st May 1917

WAR DIARY
or
INTELLIGENCE SUMMARY.
(Erase heading not required.)

Army Form C. 2118.

Place	Date	Hour	Summary of Events and Information	Remarks and references to Appendices
Bergin	May 1st		Coys moved to trenches previous thurs. Bombing & Lewis gun training	
"	" 2nd		Coys at disposal of Commanders for inspection of clothing, equipment kits. Lecture given to NCOs & Coys Platoon pile in app out. General cleaning up. Lewis Gun instructors	
"	" 3rd		Coys worked & trained general for attack in trenches	
"	" 4th		Orders received to march to Old Camp Tartine & G.O.L (that 5th B.W) Battn marched & arrived Nrth of Hutts - arriving from La Crosta transp Grenadier Detachment Lewis Theme by Motor Bus & sent G.L.J.A. (Mon. St Littoen) (remainder marched & arrived there) Battn proceeded to C.C.L. the night was spent in the open owing to the overcrowded of supply to cover in the dark	
Wilchama	May 5th		Day spent in finding men & Batts & cleaning up etc. Wilch Wood - we were put in at night apples area of trenches behind Grenadiers trench - the men were of these knew we should than the 15th June 1915 2 NCOs killed & 1 march & 6 OR wounded	
"	" 6th		Trenches working parties Lieut J ——— wounded. Trenches cont to receive enemy shell fire wounded	
"	" 7th		Heavy raining by German *Minnen* or *Trench Mortars* inflicting bombarded on *Wilchara* or trench *Jammery* Capt J Pendleton J. R. & 50 hour wounded Lieut victim *Grenadier* L OR wounded	
"	" 8th		Now on take a 9th Bn addition to have caused by afternoon Casualties 14 p + 268 wounded	

Army Form C. 2118.

WAR DIARY
or
INTELLIGENCE SUMMARY.
(Erase heading not required.)

Instructions regarding War Diaries and Intelligence Summaries are contained in F. S. Regs., Part II. and the Staff Manual respectively. Title pages will be prepared in manuscript.

Place	Date	Hour	Summary of Events and Information	Remarks and references to Appendices
Old German Trenches (G.6.b.) (SB.N.W.)	May 9th		Camp routine on 8th	
	10		Rifle inspection & kit have ready by Officers. Men resting & ready at night	Casualties 1 wounded
	11		Rifle inspection & cleaning of equipment. Lectures & lessons to the remaining officers & men not in the trenches	Casualties
			Officers set working party at night to fill ammunition, rations, water, etc	2 O.R. wounded
	12th		Same routine as 8th	Cas of 12th in mining
	13th		" "	
	14th		" "	
	15th		Rifle inspection & lecture reading by officers. Men working party at night	
	16th		" & one Lewis gun section reducing one Lewis Bombing and 1 Officers' reconnoitring patrol & night working on Red line	
	17th		Rifle inspection & Lectures & men marching by officers. Men working party	
	18th		" Lectures etc. Evening relieving party on red line at night	3 O.R. wounded
	19th		" & half hour musketry & afternoon	2 O.R wounded
	20		Batt. moved out of Reserve and moved from Old German trenches – G.6.b. at 6.15 and bivouaced at St Patrick's G.15.c	

WAR DIARY
or
INTELLIGENCE SUMMARY.
(Erase heading not required.)

Army Form C. 2118.

Instructions regarding War Diaries and Intelligence Summaries are contained in F. S. Regs., Part II. and the Staff Manual respectively. Title pages will be prepared in manuscript.

Place	Date	Hour	Summary of Events and Information	Remarks and references to Appendices
Witternes	21st	6.45 9.45	Parade 5.3. 6.45 9.45 August drill & two hours Lewis gun instruct: & two hours tactical exercises in the morning. 2nd Lt B Allen ... Lewis gun course ...	
			A working party on hours of 1 N.C.O. + 54 O.R. per company to work ...	
			Water + wet pine lines.	
	22nd		Rewing + Batt at noon 2nd Division ... last outfitted	
	23rd		on ... moving to ... the trenches. Bath platoons to ... A ...	
			Battalion Orders No. 26 (652) A working party as provided ... No 2 Coy ... of Cot ...	
			... for G.3.1 ... after the ... part left Batt moved at 11 a.t.	
Vincent Mine	24th		... of ... camp Officers and Sirs Buckley + Hay in ... of 4 Companies &	
"8.a"			Headquarters ... Oceans, Sergts + Standly ... (below & fair. Washing only)	
(safe ant)	25th		Working party provided as in the 9.0+	1 OR wounded
	26th		Corps ... Coy Commanders	(name to be rung)
	27th		Foot Inspection 8 am Church Parade 10.30	
	28th		Adjutant having Musketry, Bombing + Lewis gun instruction	
	29th		Usual Batt Parties. Also the respirators when tested & gas tended. Afternoon Contest Strung +	
			Bank Holiday	

WAR DIARY
or
INTELLIGENCE SUMMARY.

Army Form C. 2118.

Place	Date	Hour	Summary of Events and Information	Remarks and references to Appendices
Bethune	May 30th		Morning. O.T. Rifle practice further under Batt'n 3 rds. grouping & 10 rds. rapid. Afternoon lectures to Officers standing (fires) & Lewis machines & Lewis gun. Battn practice landing in trench etc. bomb use. Bayonet fencing in pairs & have instructions in throwing gun to one too beyond trench.	
Bethune	May 31st		Morning. O.T. [illegible] Training in close from bombing, musketry & bayonet fighting. In the evening Bn Comd. ordered down to Bruillard to instruct the trainees & support to be taken over by the Battn on the next evening.	

1/6/17

[signature] Lt. Col.
Comm'd 7th Gurkhas OC.

CONFIDENTIAL

Vol 13

WAR DIARY

of

NELSON BATTN. — 189th INFANTRY BRIGADE

63rd (ROYAL NAVAL) DIVISION

from
1st June 1917
to
30th June 1917

[signature]
Lt. COLONEL
Commanding
NELSON BATTN

1st July 1917

Army Form C. 2118.

Nelson Batt[n]

WAR DIARY
or
INTELLIGENCE SUMMARY.
(Erase heading not required.)

Instructions regarding War Diaries and Intelligence Summaries are contained in F. S. Regs., Part II. and the Staff Manual respectively. Title pages will be prepared in manuscript.

Place	Date	Hour	Summary of Events and Information	Remarks and references to Appendices
Ocklincourt Area Road & Schofield camp	June 1st		Physical training, cleaning up & gear prior to moving to the line. In the evening Coy moved off midnight to relieve the 2/4 R.B. 2 Coy's (H & B) & Head qrs in Pty. Starting at B.21, C.43. 1 Coy at B.176, C.B, 1 Coy at B.15,0	
Oppy Trench (B.P.1,C. Ballieul)	" 2nd		Batt in Support. 2 Coy on Working parties at night	
	" 3rd		- do -	
	" 4th		- do -	
Front Line	" 5th		Batt relieved the Hawke in the line. West and S.W. of Oppy. 3 Coy's in Front line One Coy in close support (Line B.18,a, 3.0 to 24, C, 5.14)	
Hawke	" 6th		- do - - do -) Our artillery very active on German front line and support	
Oppy	" 7th		Batt in line 3 Coy's in front line, 1 Coy in support	
	" 8th		- do -	
	" 9th		- do -	
	" 10th		- do - - do - Relieved night of 10/11 July	
Ocklincourt " 11th			The East Lancs (11th) Spent in cleaning up and improving billets	
B.28.a.6.14	" 12th		3 Coy on Working party at night (on Gun & Long trench)	
B.C.S.A. old German line	" 13th		Moved H Old German line, 3 Coy on Working parties at night (on Gun & Long trench)	
	" 14th		123 O.R. carrying for 176 Tunnelling Coy (at night). Men not on working party + P.T. & service gun instruction	

Army Form C. 2118.

WAR DIARY
or
INTELLIGENCE SUMMARY.
(Erase heading not required.)

Nelson Bath

Place	Date	Hour	Summary of Events and Information	Remarks and references to Appendices
Boddincourt June 5 G.34 d German do			O.R. carrying parties at night for 176 Tunnelling Coy. Men not on night work at P.T. Gymnastics and individual and extended order training.	
	"16		-do- -do- -do-	
	"17		Church Parade in morning and Carrying parties at night. Training done during day.	
	"18		Whole Bath. on carrying parties for 176 Tunnelling Coy and 100 men Lun. Coy.	
	"19		-do- -do-	
	"20		Officers and N.C.O.s not on working party or previous nights reserved Instruction on Lewis Gun & Bombing etc. Carrying parties on previous night	
	"21		187th Bde stoke Mortar Shafts. 100 men carrying for 176th Tunnelling Coy. Night 100 men carrying for 176 Tunnelling Coy and 18.0th Tunnelling Coy.	
Maroeuil "22 27 & 63			Bath. moved to Maroeuil F.276. 6.3. (51°N.E.) Left Bodincourt 8.45 A.M. Lewis Coys taken over from Franc Bath. at 11 A.M. 200 men on walking party. previous night arrived in Maroeuil Bath. training 6.30 to 10-30 A.M. Full Strength Gas at 6 P.M.	
(51.G.N.E.) "23				
"24			Bn: inspection. Church Parade 11 A.M. No training during day	
"25			Rudely (3rd Army Range) in the morning. Whole Bath. Staffed at Bath Maroeuil in afternoon	
"26			Rudely (Living on Range) in the morning. The Fst, 2nd formation were drilled. Training in Relief of garrisons and reconnaissance. by 2nd in C.	(49th Div dividing trench works)
"27			Lewis Gunners firing on Range - remainder of Bath. on L.G. 1st Tan. Presentation of Medals by G.O.C. 10 A.M. Whole Bath. listening to M.E.O. & C.O. of officers by G.S. & Companies	
"28			in evening, Reinforcement. Joined Bath. no Service. Church Parade & Sunday. 6.30 & 8.30 Lewis Gunners firing on Range - 2nd Phase of Attack carried over the open - accompanied by 2nd Coy of whole Bath. loading in Bath. Demonstration - All Officers attended. Demonstration - Wind storm & Dusk Bath.	
"29			6.30-9.30 Lewis Gunners firing on Range - remainder. Bombing and Hundely 10-0 A.M. 31st & 2nd Phase of Attack - consolidation of position. 3.30-5.30 2nd Brees.	

Army Form C. 2118.

Nelson Bttn

WAR DIARY
or
INTELLIGENCE SUMMARY.
(Erase heading not required.)

Place	Date	Hour	Summary of Events and Information	Remarks and references to Appendices
Beaucourt (76.b.6.3) (51.G.N.E.)	June 30th		All 4 Coys lying on Barge - Hfflication Shob in Goo Helmet. 10.30 9th 4 the 14th Bn complete by two Coys on a frontage of 300 yds. Extending from Artillery formation and advancing similar objective & sectional rushes, final stages taking & sections for Hank and crossfire . forbid Garrisons. Remaining two Coys unaffected of operations until ordered at dawn.	

Frank Levin
Lt Colonel
A/ Commanding "NELSON BATTN."

SECRET

WAR DIARY

OF

NELSON BATTALION

189th Infantry Brigade.

FROM 1st July 1917.
TO 31st July 1917.

Fredk Lewis Lieut. Colonel
Commanding Nelson Bn
189th Infantry Bde.

Army Form C. 2118.

WAR DIARY
or
INTELLIGENCE SUMMARY.
(Erase heading not required.)

NELSON BATT.ⁿ

Instructions regarding War Diaries and Intelligence Summaries are contained in F. S. Regs., Part II. and the Staff Manual respectively. Title pages will be prepared in manuscript.

Place	Date	Hour	Summary of Events and Information	Remarks and references to Appendices
RDEUIL	July 1st		Church parade. 13 Reinforcement joined Battⁿ	
2/6.6-3 T CNE.	2		Training. Bugars practised in US attack. (open warfare) Bathing afternoon	
	3		Training - Cleaning - Inspecting prior to moving forward. C.O.⁴ Coronel's visit support line system (RED LINE)	
T. SUPPORT Tⁿ	4		Marched from Camp 7.AM. They have held behind rest of A 24d Moved up TOMMY ALLEY at 1/pm. Tⁿ moving interval between companies. Drew A.B Mg C.D. Reviewed 1st CHESHIRE Regt at SUGAR POST B16d	
SUGAR POST NW B16d			Recn empire 3.45pm Trunks moved overnight. Situation normal - Night - Shelling Ration parties only at night - 1 OR wounded Front line Batt HOOD Right - HAWKE left - NELSON support	
	5.		Situation quiet - 12 Reinforcements joined. 5 pm. support 2 from Rest Camp A.T.C. Coy worked front line. R+D improving support line. Casualties 1. OR wounded	
	6.		C.O. and 5 officers obtained acknowledge and list trenches at Rodincourt. Situation Quiet. R+D worked front line. H.C. Support line 12 Reinforcement rejoined from hospital & Orange. Sub die Couture wounded. Sick. Casualties 1. OR wounded	
	7.		Situation normal & artillery both sides quiet. A+B worked front line & communication. C+D support. Casualties nil.	
	8.		Situation Quiet. Hostile artillery fairly active - work on trenches by companies as before. 1. OR killed 2. OR wounded	
	9.		Situation and work by ft getration	

WAR DIARY
or
INTELLIGENCE SUMMARY

Army Form C. 2118.

Place	Date	Hour	Summary of Events and Information	Remarks and references to Appendices
FRONT LINE OPPY	Jan 10		Bombarded Ridge of HAWKE Rd in front line (Lerr-Batt) at 5.30pm. B & C. front lines C & D Support Relief complete 12.30pm. Stretcher Street. Lt Buckle slightly wounded remained at duty. 1 OR	
	11		Men 7 wounded. 2 Reinforcement joined "B".	
	12		Situation front Quiet. Enemy T.M's active - slow progress. 1 OR killed	
			Previous entries, Bombs dropped in right front C.o's by Hostile Aircraft. Two pilots out and working on heights. 8 OR wounded	
	13		Quiet & enemy artillery active during night - working front line. Engine active but occasional MG applied. Zenith Cemetery. 1 OR wounded. Coy's 3 offices Lt Col & Lewis D.S.O went in leave.	
	14		Evening very heavy shelling by enemy 4.2 & 5.5. Supposed heavy anger - work continues. Relieving. A relieved B and D relieved C. 1 OR wounded. 1 OR killed	
	15		Normal situation during day. Work on trouble trenches of Henry Lane. Intent MG's and dugouts in front. Rain. Artillery Quiet. Casualties 1 OR wounded. 2.0pm general bombardment.	
	16		V. heavy bombardment of enemy on LEFT 1.0-2.30 AM. enemy counter bombardment slight. I know his Gas Scouts wounded. Relieved by 1st Somm & 13" Gloucester. Forms my left Relief not complete until next day.	
	17		Relief complete 11.10 AM. Battalion moved to HAZEBIELD Camp. (Anjum Region) Cleaning & inspection. B. to billets.	
	18		Companies inspected by C.O (Major Ruther) R.M. Lane Marque expenses. C. & D & 1pl. B working parts for R.E. A. to Baths.	

Army Form C. 2118.

WAR DIARY
or
INTELLIGENCE SUMMARY.
(Erase heading not required.)

Instructions regarding War Diaries and Intelligence Summaries are contained in F. S. Regs., Part II. and the Staff Manual respectively. Title pages will be prepared in manuscript.

Place	Date	Hour	Summary of Events and Information	Remarks and references to Appendices
SEAFIELD CAMP	July 19		Companies training. D Co. Recruits. A+C inspect S. Co. Battn military Cinema in afternoon. Orders received at 10.45pm to stand by ready to move at 15 minutes notice.	
R.N.W.	20		Order to move by cancelled. Specialist + Platoon training continued. Officers attended Cinema at Musselburgh of Q.O.C. Bns. Cpls. commanded parade.	
.C.S.B.	21		Normal training, Drills + musketry on 25 yd range.	
	22		Church Parade. Relieved by Hants Bt + moved to billets at ST AUBIN, accompanied by 1 mule & R.M band. Arrived 6.10pm. St Aubin? T. Paris joined.	
	23		Training - Reorganisation of platoon - Field drill + training. P.T.+B.F. firing. 16 O.R. rejoined	
	24		Training no. 4 Scheme. Platoon drill + training. One company firing new musketry course Coy. examination of practice. Drill + specialist training.	
	25			
	26		Coy. 5 yd. Company training. The company fired new musketry course on 200 yd range. drill.	
	27			
	28		All companies fired 5 rounds at 400 yds. 3 Minor parades. 2nd Bn Cage Mann + Stevenson completed B.F. musketry course. Church parade.	
	29			
	30		Training in morning. B.E. Nelson 1st R.M's at #1 C.67. Bgade Recon. Right sector of Divl front. Relief	
H.C.67.	31		operations - 7.45pm. Garment training + N.C.O's class. D Co. training. Rest & No C Co. sewage operation. Lectures for all officers. m. May Richey + Simpson visited by Major Sutton.	

Hugh Lewin? Lt Col.
Command? Nelson Battn 188 "Bryan?"

Army Form C. 2118.

WAR DIARY
or
INTELLIGENCE SUMMARY.
(Erase heading not required.)

NELSON BATTⁿ

AUGUST 1917.

Place	Date	Hour	Summary of Events and Information	Remarks and references to Appendices
S DE LA NISON DINCHE	August 1st 1917		Training Spare Lewis Gun teams. Sub Lt Spooner. N.C.O's class under 2nd Comdr Price. 6 Coy made permanent supply party for Tony Alley under Sub Lt Dawson. A Coy working on Salvage Area.	9/1/15
	2nd		6 Coy wiring the Red Line. Lecture to Officers by Major Barker. 30's proceeded on leave. Training continued. D Coy working on Salvage Area. A Coy wiring the Red Line. Reinforcements 15 O.R. Lecture to Officers by Major Barker.	
	3rd		Training continued. D Coy wiring Red Line. Officers lecture by Major Barker. Surgeon returned from Starforth, production Special leave from A.D.M.S. Capt Cant R.A.M.C. returned to 149th Field Ambulance. 6 Coy working on Salvage area. Lt Middleton returned from leave.	
	4th		Training continued. Lecture to Officers by 2nd in Command. A Coy provide detachment 25 men for upkeep of Tony. A Coy working on Salvage area. 6 Coy wiring Red Line.	
	5th		Training continued. 25 O.R's rejoin Battⁿ from Rod Markoib. Lecture to Officers by 2nd in Command. D coy's went on Salvage. 6 Coy's wiring Red Line	
	6th		Training continued. 27 O.R's rejoin B Coy from T.M.B. working party working party of 300 men from A.C & D Coy's working from 1pm - 3am on burned cable trench near Gautzeur Road by Brown House.	
	7th		Specialist Training continued. Other stand off. Sub Lt Batchelor proceeded on leave.	

WAR DIARY or INTELLIGENCE SUMMARY

Army Form C. 2118.

NELSON BATT   AUGUST 1917

Place	Date	Hour	Summary of Events and Information	Remarks and references to Appendices
HAMISON	7th		Working party 200 O.Rs continue work on Buried Cable Trench which is completed.	
BLANGY	8th		The 189th Inf Bde. Relieved by 188th Inf Bde. in not sub-sector – 189th Bde relieves 190th Bde in the left sub-sector of our front. The Batt'n relieved the 1st Batt'n Royal Fusiliers in the front line. – Nelson B Coy relieved Nelson B & C Coys 7th R.F. on the right. Nelson C in Subs relieved a Coy of Artists Rifles attached to 7th R.F. in training. Nelson D on left relieved A & D Coys R.F. A Coy Nelson relieved 1 Pl of all four Coys R.F. in Support in RAILWAY TRENCH & MARINETTE STREET.	
	9th		Day quiet. Enemy artillery active at night shelling BRADFORD TRENCH and ROTTEN ROW, junction of Railway MT & R. ALLEY. Sub Lt TOWKER accidentally wounded in knee from shot in HOOD ALLEY as he was returning from Patrol.	
	10th		Day quiet. A/S BARKER to England for commission. 11.30 pm hostile bombardment of Bradford TRENCH intermittent shelling & m/g gun fire during night.	
	11th		Day very quiet. 11 ORs reinforcements arrived. Heavy shelling of BROWN & CHARING X at 3.50 pm.	
	12th		Day quiet – Artillery barrage opened for 5 mins on CHARING ST ROAD at 4.30 am. Two ORs of C Coy killed –	
	13th		Day quiet. Intermittent artillery fire during night. Barrage opened on C Coy front line	

Army Form C. 2118.

WAR DIARY
or
INTELLIGENCE SUMMARY.
(Erase heading not required.)

Army 1917   NELSON Batt.

Place	Date	Hour	Summary of Events and Information	Remarks and references to Appendices
Suez Canal Defences in front	Aug 13		at 12.5 am 2 ORs killed 5 ORs wounded. 12 fao shells fired on ration dump at 12.30 am.	
	14th		Intermittent shelling during day. at 6.30 am 7.15 am & 10.30 pm heavy bombardment of Support & reserve lines by 4.2s & 5.9s. Each burst lasting about 5 mins. 5 ORs leave to England. 1 OR wounded (Oldfield)	
	15th		Activity below normal. Only slight shelling. Sub Lt BAXTER wounded in arm on patrol.	
	16th		Activity below normal. 3 ORs reinforcements from CDTD. 30 ORs from base - our artillery active. Batt's relieved by the ARTISTS RIFLES. relief complete 9.45 pm.	
3 REY CAMP	17th		Batts moved into HOREY CAMP. All in by 1 am. Cleaning up. Company rifle & hut Inspections. Batt's rifles & Lewis guns inspected by the North Armourer. Bathes at Ct Kubbannee. Training commenced 9 – 12 am	
	18th		Church parade with Hood Battn. 20 ORs reinforcements from base arrived.	
	19th		Training continued. 2nd RN & SB Rifles played in Camp. Speedwell 2 – 3 pm	
	20th		4 ORs arrived from C.D.T.D	
	21st		Training continued. French & French Officers. Range & R.G. & Combined Musketry Course Fathes de Doi Cinema - at 3 pm.	

WAR DIARY
or
INTELLIGENCE SUMMARY.

Army Form C. 2118.

(Erase heading not required.)

August 1917.   NEZ.SPR. Aug. 1918.

Place	Date	Hour	Summary of Events and Information	Remarks and references to Appendices
AUBREY CAMP.	Aug 22nd		Training continued. Franni Brucel played in Camp. Night operation in GAS respirators.	
	23rd		Training continued. No training in afternoon - Brigade Sports in BETHUNE CMR Bulps hope 9 players Black Coms? in Div Theatre. 23 OR reinforcements arrived from base.	
H.T. Sec iv	24th		Stood off in training for company inspection and parade at St Catherine at 7 pm paraded to relieve ANSON Battn in support line of Bn Battalion in NEUVR & MARES TRENCH. B. C. D Coys in that trench relieved B A C Coys respt. A Coy NELSON relieved D Coy ANSON in REDLINE at BLOC Post. Night quiet.	
	25th		Day + night quiet. 2nd Lt WRIGHT reported for duty as Transport Officer. Battn found working parties on LITTLE MILLY. TOWY. NEWL 1 BROUGH. trenches.	
	26th		Day + night quiet. working parties as on 25th.	
	27th		Day + night quiet. 3 OR.s Reinforcements arrived. working parties as above. 2nd/POPLAR ALLEY new target off PLARN	
	28th		Day + night quiet. (R/S Col Steno to command bde. Major Barker assumed command of Battn) 18.109 OR reinforcements arrived from CBTD. working parties as above + running fronts for T.H. Bueno Lin. SubLt BATCHELOR to command 8 Coy vice 2ndLt CREWFORD Ka 1250	
	29th		Day + night quiet. minifre needs posted to Coys. A33. B32. C37. D47. remain at transit under Sub Lt CREWFORD. 1 Ruppeling + Major Working parties as on 25th. lens buts in BROUGH ALLEY cancelled. Several orderment of CRUMPET TRENCH freed for fire in the To Sener	

WAR DIARY or INTELLIGENCE SUMMARY

Army Form C. 2118.

Place: **NELSON BATT'N**
Month: **August 1917**

Place	Date	Hour	Summary of Events and Information	Remarks and references to Appendices
N.A.L. TRENCH	Aug 30		Day & night quiet. Bombardment of CRUMPET Trench cancelled. 51 OR reinforcements arrive from C.D.D. remain at transport lines under 2nd Lt CRAWFORD. E.G.G. Mjor P.O.S. BLOGG & KILGHORN N.Coy and KA/hy CHAMBERS B.Coy - finding in all ratio hot guard.	
	3/35		Bombardment of CRUMPET TRENCH commenced at 8am with 18 pndr. Heavies commenced at C.Coy withdraw to Reserve 7am. D Coy Relief up to C.Coy 20/07. Sub Lt H Cooper wounded at 2.30am Referring 10.45am. Bombardment ceased at 4pm. Sub Lt H Cooper ER Batts worked on TOWL WALL	
			TRENCH off NEW EAST NAVAL TRENCHES & RED LINE	New trench maps issued November 1917

CONFIDENTIAL.   NELSON BN.

WAR DIARY

FROM

1st September, 1917.

To.

30th September, 1917.

To HQ:
189th Inf Bde.

H Reed Lt + Adjt
for Lieut. Col.
Commanding NELSON Bn.

Army Form C. 2118.

WAR DIARY
or
INTELLIGENCE SUMMARY.
(Erase heading not required.)

SEPTEMBER NELSON Batt⁴

Place	Date	Hour	Summary of Events and Information	Remarks and references to Appendices
NAVAL TRENCH	1st		Intermittent Enemy shelling during night. 1 O.R. wounded. Batt⁴ relieved by DRAKE Batt⁴ & moved into the Ry Cutting. A Coy NELSON relieved by C Coy DRAKE. B Coy by D Coy & D Coy by B Coy NELSON & C Coy moving out independently at dusk. Relief complete 10.50 pm.	
RAILWAY CUTTING	2nd		185 reinforcements joined the Batt⁴ from the Transport Lines. Work on improving shelters & shelters in the Cutting. B & C Coy Batt⁴s POCLINCOURT. 5 OR reinforcements from Base & O.R. reinforcements from R.M. & C.O.T.D joined Batt⁴.	
"	3rd		Work continued in cutting. A&D Coy Batt⁴s PUCLINCOURT. 2 O.Rs to Rest Camp.	
"	4th		The 63rd (RN) Division Relieved as far as Junction of HABERT & BAAY TRENCHES. NELSON Batt⁴ relieved the 1st MANCHS in C.I. Sub Sectr renamed RH Sub Sectr. Guides met A Coy at Junction S. DUKE ST & DUSK at 10 am. LEFT FRONT D Coy NELSON relieved A Coy MARSBALKS. RIGHT FRONT A Coy NELSON relieved B Coy M².SK³. SUPPORT B Coy Nelson relieved C Coy M².SK³. RESERVE C Coy Nelson relieved Hd Qrts Batt⁴ in REDLINE between BUSH & RAILWAY. Relief complete 2 am. Night quiet no casualties. Work wiring FRONT improving parapets & Dugouts	
RH Sub Sec	5th		Hostile Artillery quiet day & night. M/C guns active at night & some shelling of RATIN DUMP at RAILWAY S. DUKE ST. work A&D Coy wiring the front. B Coy improving MARQUIS & carrying for A&D.C Coy work in RED LINE & new Com. post on FERN SUPPORT & improvement of Hd Q & Duke St.	
	6th		Enemy trench mortars active. Some shelling of ratin dump. 2nd Lt BURLSSON joined Batt⁴ as Transport O. Reported Batt⁴ Hd Qr Hd 7⁴ Work continued as on 5⁴	

Army Form C. 2118.

WAR DIARY
or
INTELLIGENCE SUMMARY.
(Erase heading not required.)

Instructions regarding War Diaries and Intelligence Summaries are contained in F. S. Regs., Part II. and the Staff Manual respectively. Title pages will be prepared in manuscript.

NELSON Battn.

SEPTEMBER

Place	Date	Hour	Summary of Events and Information	Remarks and references to Appendices
R4.	Sept 7th		6 OR reinforcements joined Battn from XIII & Corps D.T.D. Hostile trench mortars active	
R.b. Sector	8th		8 OR reinforcements joined Battn from XIII & Corps D.T.D. Enemy quiet during the day. Heavy bombardment of ration dumps with 5.9" at about 9.15pm. One platoon up with direct hit 400 yds from railhead. Fighting patrol under Sub Lt. TAYLOR with Sub Lt. DOLMAN + 25 ORs endeavoured to raid enemy post at N.E.S.T. end of FRESNOY TRENCH. Sub Lt. TAYLOR and 7 ORs wounded - 2 slightly.	
	9th		Day & night quiet.	
	10th		Day quiet. Battn relieved by 7th Battn Royal Fusiliers at 3pm. D Coy NELSON 2 left platoons by D Coy R.F. right platoon by 6 Coy R.F. A Coy NELSON left platoon by C Coy R.F. 2 right plns by A Coy R.F. B Coy NELSON by B Coy R.F. C Coy NELSON by 4th Bed. Regt. Relief complete 6.30 pm. Battn proceeded to billets in MAROEUIL by march route. Halt in ROCLINCOURT for hot meal.	
MAROEUIL	11th		13 OR reinforcements arrived from base. Baths. Lts Lt G. MEDNER + SUB LT CRAWFORD on leave	
AUBREY CAMP	12th		Battn moved by march route to AUBREY CAMP. leaving MAROEUIL 4.30 pm.	
	13th		6 ORs. Surplus instructional staff reported from XIIIth C.D.T.D. also for reinforcements from base.	
	14th		B. D Coys training. A+C Coy working parties 104 ORs per company working in RED LINE by night.	
	15th		A. C. + B Coys training. D Coy 104 OR working party in RED LINE. A+B Coys training. B Coy working party at night. Bde School. C Coy working parties a.m. in RED LINE.	

Army Form C. 2118.

WAR DIARY
or
INTELLIGENCE SUMMARY.
(Erase heading not required.)

SEPTEMBER. NELSON BATT&

Instructions regarding War Diaries and Intelligence Summaries are contained in F. S. Regs., Part II and the Staff Manual respectively. Title pages will be prepared in manuscript.

Place	Date	Hour	Summary of Events and Information	Remarks and references to Appendices
UBREY	Sept. 15th		Scheme at NAGUNLIEU. C.O. 2/L. in C[ommand] & Adjt attended. 3pm. lecture to Officers & N.C.O's in cooperation between Infantry & Air Service. Sub Lieuts REED & CONELLY joined the Batt posted to D & B Coys respectively.	
N.M.P.	16th		D. Coy working party am. A Coy at night. Church parade 10am and H.Q. O/C. noon. Officers & N.C.O.S	
	17th		Visit to Aerodrome. Flight by C[ommandin]g Officer. Sub Lt ARNOLD & P.O. ARSCOT. Lts GRANT TRATERS joined Batt. Sub Lts JEHRING, BIGGS & BEAUMONT form P[ost] Army School. C[omman]d[in]g Officer to RANGALAH. TORPEDO demonstration Batt moved to ROUND HAY CAMP Morng at 2pm.	
ROUNDHAY			5 O.Rs reinforcement joined from base & 10 ORs from base	
A.M.P.	18th		Training in WIRING & general. B.C.D. Coys working by night on wiring GAVRELLE VILLAGE. 30 Rs reinforcements joined from base depot. 6ORs on leave	
	19th		A Coy Cutting grass am. wiring GAVRELLE continued. A.C.& D Coys working 1 O.R. (2/Lt m'C[ormac]k) accidentally wounded wiring B Coy Baths at Bellincourt	
	20th		A.B.& D Coys WIRING GAVRELLE. C Coy Baths at Bellincourt	
	21st		A B & C Coys WIRING GAVRELLE. D Coy Baths at Richmont	
	22nd		B. C & D. Coys WIRING GAVRELLE. A Coy Baths at Richmont	
	23rd		A. B & C. Coys WIRING G. AVRELLE.	
	24th		Inspection of the Batt by Rear Admiral Division. Sub Lt Crawford returned from leave. 1st Platoon from Service. 158th Inf. Bd. relieved by 142nd Bde of 47th Division. Nelson Battn relieved by 1/15 London Regt & proceeded by train from CHANTELLER to ECOIVRES & by bus from ECOIVRES to TINQUES	
	25th			

WAR DIARY
or
INTELLIGENCE SUMMARY

Army Form C. 2118.

NELSON BATT.

Place	Date	Hour	Summary of Events and Information	Remarks and references to Appendices
TRÔNES	Sept 25th		Batt⁰ billetted in TRÔNES. 45 O.R.s rejoined Batt⁰ from Travelling Coy.	
	26th		Coy Inspections.	
	27th		Training commenced. Sub Lts OKERR & PAGE rejoined Batt⁰ from HM Corps DID Ponds. 135 ORs	
	28th		Joined Batt⁰. Reinforcements 107 from repairs. Gains 26 ORs & 2 from hosps.)	
	29th		Training continued. Inter platoon football matches begun. A⁰11 9th beat N⁰16. 4q⁰ beat N⁰5 - 9½.	
			Training continued. Sub Lt HOWARD joined Batt⁰ from England. N⁰10 R⁵ beat N⁰15 - N⁰12 R⁵ beat	
	30th		N⁰3. N⁰19 & N⁰8 draw.	
		9 am	Church parade.	

Ned Weir
OC Nelson Bn

Bob
OC Nelson Bn

CONFIDENTIAL

NELSON BATTALION

Vol 17

WAR DIARY

From

1st October, 1917.

To

31st October, 1917.

Stuart G. Jones
Lt. Cmdr. RNVR
Cmdg. NELSON Bn.

To H.Q.
189th Inf Bde.

WAR DIARY or INTELLIGENCE SUMMARY.

Army Form C. 2118.

NELSON BATTN.

OCTOBER

Place	Date	Hour	Summary of Events and Information	Remarks and references to Appendices
INGUES	1st		Training continued. Lieut H.L. Reed detached to 189th Bgde H.Q. Sub-Lieut Bird joined the Battn from England.	
	2nd		Battn. less C Coy. left billeting area at 7.15 p.m. and marched to SAVY where entrainment was completed by 11 p.m.	
	3rd		C. Coy left Tincques at 11 a.m. and entrained at SAVY. Battn detrained at PROVEN at 9.15 a.m. and moved off at 11.45 a.m. for NOUVEAU MONDÉ (Sheet 27. Edition 2 - D5, D14, D15) where they went into billets at 3 p.m.	
NOUVEAU MONDE	4th		C Coy arrived in billets at 5.30 a.m. Platoon training continued. Class assembled for training of Scouts and Observers for each Platoon. Two reinforcements arrived from England, two from the Base, and sixty-nine from the 10th Entrenching Battn.	
	5th		Battalion moved by bus from Nouveau Monde to Brown Camp (Sheet 28, A22 d & 5)	
	6th		Battalion moved by march from Brown Camp to	

WAR DIARY
INTELLIGENCE SUMMARY.

(Erase heading not required.)

NELSON. BATT^{n.}

OCTOBER

Army Form C. 2118.

Place	Date	Hour	Summary of Events and Information	Remarks and references to Appendices
REIGERS-BURG.	6th.		to REIGERSBURG CAMP at 3 p.m. (Sheet 28. B 30. c. 54.) and bivouacs were made.	
	7th.		600 men from Battⁿ employed in prolonging Light Railway beyond St Julien. Remainder improved bivouacs. Training: Improvement of bivouacs.	
	8th.		Training.	
	9th.		Training.	
	10th.		Four companies in two reliefs engaged in road construction at C22 d S.S. (Sheet 28. 7.w.)	
	11th.		Work continued as on the 10th. A Party of Officers and N.C.O.s visited the XVIII th Corps model ground. Casualties. - S.O.R.	
	12th.		Three companies continued work under R.E.s. C. Coy moved as advanced party to Kemptin Park (B 15. b.3.5.) to erect shelters for the Battⁿ. Casualties - 2.O.R. Lieut. A.W. Buckle detached to XIXth Corps Training Dept.	
KEMPTON PARK.	13th.		Battⁿ moved to KEMPTON PARK. (Sheet 28. C.15. b.3.5.) A Coy continued erecting shelters. B.C. & D continued work under R.E.s.	

WAR DIARY
or
INTELLIGENCE SUMMARY.

NELSON. BATT^N. OCTOBER

Army Form C. 2118.

Place	Date	Hour	Summary of Events and Information	Remarks and references to Appendices
EMPTON PARK.	13th.		Casualties – 2 O.R. wounded.	
	14th.		Work continued. 14th. Capt Stanford C.F. joined Batt. from D.A.C. Camp bombed by hostile aircraft at 1.10 a.m. and shelled throughout the night. Casualties from bomb – 2.O.R. wounded. Casualties on working parties – 2 O.R. killed. 8 O.R. wounded.	
	15th.		Work continued. Lieut H Howard evacuated wounded. Casualties. 1 O.R. wounded, 1 O.R. wounded to duty.	
	16th.		Work continued. Casualties – 6 O.R. wounded.	
	17th.		Work continued. Lieut E.V. Sardine evacuated wounded. Casualties – 2 O.R. killed, 4 O.R. wounded, 2 O.R. wounded to duty.	
	18th.		Work continued.	
	19th.		Work continued. Casualties. 1 O.R. wounded.	
BRIQUE CAMP.	20th.		Work continued. Casualties 1 O.R. wounded, 1 O.R. wounded to duty. Batt. moved to La Brique Camp (C.26.d C.5.h. Sh. Julien 28 NW 2.)	
	21st.		Work continued	
	22nd.		Work continued. Casualties: T/Lieut P. Bachelor wounded. 4 O.R. killed	

WAR DIARY or INTELLIGENCE SUMMARY

Army Form C. 2118.

NELSON BATTⁿ. OCTOBER

Place	Date	Hour	Summary of Events and Information	Remarks and references to Appendices
A BRIGDE.	22nd		8. O.R. wounded.	
	23rd		Battⁿ moved at 9 a.m. to BRAKE. CAMP. (Sheet 28 NW. A.30.C.)	
BRAKE CAMP.	24th		Parades and inspections. Sub Lieut Stringfield rejoined from Div. H.Q.	
	25th		Parades and inspections. A Party of Officers, N.C.O's, and runners reconnoitred the forward area.	
	26th		Preparation for moving into the line	
	27th		Battⁿ moved at 10 a.m. to IRISH CAMP and thence at dusk to the line to relieve the HOOD BATTⁿ. D Coy took up a position 300 yards east of VARLET FARM, with one platoon of A Coy on their right next to the Canadian Corps. A Coy held a line extending north west from the Cemetery 300 yards south of WALLEMOLEN to the road running from INCH HOUSES & WALLEMOLEN, at V.27 d 6.0. C Coy held a line running north west from the same road at D3 b.19 and turning in front of INCH HOUSES to V.27 C.84. B Coy were in Sup/OP at D3 B 1.8.	

WAR DIARY or INTELLIGENCE SUMMARY

Army Form C. 2118.

Place: NELSON BATTN **OCTOBER**

Date	Hour	Summary of Events and Information	Remarks
26th		During the night the enemy was machine gunning. Sub Lieut Johnson was killed on patrol. D Coy assisted in means of large offensive patrols. Captured a Pill Box, seventy five yards in front of Flers line at V 28 c 6.4. Battalion was afterwards relieved by Artist Rifles. Casualties 2 ORs killed, 2 ORs wounded.	
29th		1 OR killed. 33 ORs wounded. 5 ORs missing. Battalion rested at Irish Camp. Lt Col Lewis and Surgeon Stafford evacuated sick. At 5.1 pm A & D Companies moved into reserve at MOOSETRAP TRENCH.	
30th		B Coy employed Stretcher bearing for 190th Brigade. A & D moved into Support in front of ALBATROSS FARM. C Company moved out to MOOSETRAP TRENCH. Casualties. 16 ORs wounded	
31st		Whole battalion moved forward to relieve various parties of 190th Brigade in the front line.	

CONFIDENTIAL

NELSON Bn
1.12.17

WAR DIARY

From

1st November 1917

To

30th November 1917

To H.Q.
189th Inf.Bde.

A/Lt Cmdr RNVR
Cmdg. NELSON Bn

WAR DIARY
INTELLIGENCE SUMMARY

Army Form C. 2118.

NELSON BATT:

Place	Date	Hour	Summary of Events and Information	Remarks and references to Appendices
TH of SPRIET.	1917 Nov		Battalion occupying line SOUTH of SPRIET in V.27 & V.28. A Coy on right, C Coy on left, D Coy immediate support & B Coy in Reserve at ALBATROSS FARM. also Headquarters. At 6.30 p.m. a party from C Coy consisting of Sub Lieut BRSARLEY and 12 O.Rs. advanced and captured enemy Pill-box at V.28.c.5.7 taking prisoner 1 Officer + 12 O.Rs. Killing 3 O.Rs. and capturing Machine Gun. Our casualties nil. Operation completed by 9 p.m. Enemy retaliation fairly heavy at 8.30. and again at 2 A.M. on 2nd	P II 1/10000
	2		Very dull day, visibility low + constant flares attract to some mins at 7 A.M. did not arrive. Enemy shelling average, intermittent machine gun fire + great activity Northern. Battalion relieved by Hood Batt at 8 p.m. relief complete by midnight.	
	3		Battalion in Brigade Reserve at CANAL BANK. On the night 2/3rd whilst the relief was taking place, three very heavy gas shellings by the enemy and the following was evacuated suffering from gas. Major BARKER, T/Lieut H.L. REED RNVR, T/Lieut F. BARRETT, T/Sub Lieut STRINGFIELD, T/Sub Lieut RICHARDSON RNVR + 50 ORs. Other casualties during the period were T/Sub Lieut APPLETON RNVR wounded, 8 ORs. 3 killed, 3 died of wounds & missing and 18 wounded. Lieut Cmdr SHELTON DSO RNVR	

Army Form C. 2118.

WAR DIARY
or
INTELLIGENCE SUMMARY.
(Erase heading not required.)

Nelson Bn.

Place	Date	Hour	Summary of Events and Information	Remarks and references to Appendices
Canal Bank	4/11/17		Battalion employed in cleaning & organisation	
	5/11/17		" moved to Dambre Camp, at 2.30 PM arrived 4 PM	
Camp	6/11/17		" entrained at 2 PM and arrived at Road Camp at 4 PM	
	7/11/17		" cleaning up	
	8/11/17		" reorganising & training	
	9/11/17		" Battal. training	
	10/11/17		" trained at 8.30 AM to Camp at Winnezeele arrived 11.45 AM. 16 men fell out	
Winnezeele	11/11/17		" left for Heisthaege at 8.40 AM arriving at 2 PM, arrived at 150	
Heisthaege	12/11/17		" May 22 men fell out	
	13/11/17		Battalion cleaning up	
	14/11/17		Platoon training. Lecture: T. C.P. Dieterle. W.B. Harrison. R.Taylor. F.A.Taylor. H.A. Bennett. 4 243 ORs arrived from reinforcement depot, on inspection they seemed to be a very fair draft, physically, & the majority of them having had no previous training in England	
	15/11/17		Platoon training	

WAR DIARY
INTELLIGENCE SUMMARY

NELSON BN

Army Form C. 2118.

Hour, Date, Place	Summary of Events and Information	Remarks and references to Appendices
STAPLES 16.11.17	Platoon training	
17.11.17	Company training	
18.11.17	Brigade Church Parade. NELSON HAWKE DRAKE Bns. Service taken by Batlst. Gwynne C.F. the Brigade left to march past G.O.C. Anson.	
19.11.17	Company training. Brigadier 189th Brigade inspected all Companies training.	
20.11.17	Company training. Subs Lieut N. Boys + 29 O.Rs reinforcements arrived.	
21.11.17	Training as usual	
22.11.17		
23.11.17	Battalion inspected by Capt O. Backhouse C.B. R.N. at Training. He was accompanied by Capt O'BACKHOUSE C.B. R.N. Lieut. F.D. PURSER, Sub Lieut T.H. COVAN (joined the Battalion)	
24.11.17	Training	
25.11.17	Church Parade	
26.11.17	Training	
27.11.17	Cleaning out training area preparatory to move	
28.11.17	Battalion left at 8.30 AM for LE NOUVEAU MONDE arriving at 2.30/m 28 attalion dusted out	
29.11.17	Battalion left LE NOUVEAU MONDE at 8.15 AM arriving at ROAD CAMP at 11.20 AM, when dusted out	
ROAD CAMP 30.11.17	Cleaning up + reorganising	

Stuart E. Jones
Lt Comdg RNVR
Comdg. NELSON Bn.

189/63 Nelson Bn 9517

WAR DIARY

INTELLIGENCE SUMMARY.

(Erase heading not required.)

Army Form C. 2118.

Place	Date	Hour	Summary of Events and Information	Remarks and references to Appendices
AD CAMP	1.12.17		Training until noon.	
	2.12.17		Church Parade. Lut A/Lt W Wellwood and Sub Lt Brearley R.N.V.R. awarded M.C. for services during operations of Nov 1 and 2nd. C.2.5603. P.O. H. Smith and R.26 A.B. J. H. Child awarded D.C.M. for services in operations as above	
	3.12.17		Company training	
	4.12.17		Company training with special reference to the employment system of attack.	
	5.12.17		Under orders to entrain and under orders to relieve 32nd Division on night of 5/6th. Orders cancelled late at night. Battn to be ready to entrain at short notice – training ceased and all ranks prepared to move.	
	6.12.17		Training continued. Operation orders for move issued by Division.	
	7.12.17		Trains cancelled – training continued.	
	8.12.17		Company training until noon. Orders for move received	
	9.12.17		Church parade. Cleaning up camp.	
CAMP BARASTRE	10.12.17		A Coy left at 1 AM remainder of Battn at 5 am, the whole were billetted in L Camp by 9 pm.	

WAR DIARY
INTELLIGENCE SUMMARY.
(Erase heading not required.)

Army Form C. 2118.

Place	Date	Hour	Summary of Events and Information	Remarks and references to Appendices
BARASTRE	11.12.17		Foot inspection and scabies inspection by M.O. Order for move received	
ETRICOURT	12.12.17		The Battalion moved from Barastre by road to Etricourt [Sheet 57d France 1/40,000] V.8. leaving BARASTRE - 12 noon, arriving ETRICOURT about 4 pm.	
	13th		Advanced party up to reconnoitre the line - Sector: (SPECIAL SHEET. PARTS OF 57d NE & SE. "NINE WOOD") LA. VACQUERIE. Squared R.9.10.15. Remainder of Batt'n moved to following area - HQ & B Coy. Q.11. - A, C & D Coys to HAVRINCOURT WOOD. Q.9. Q.14. Batt'n moved into the line - relieving 15th Royal Irish Rifles. - Time of relief 5.30 p.m. to 8.30 p.m. (36th Div. - ULSTER DIV'N)	
	14th			
	15th 16th 17th 18th		Consolidation of trenches - wiring sextchen - patrols - and cleaning out of fire and communication trenches - Duckboards found in practically all the trenches when cleaned out.	
	19th		Relieved by the Hood Battalion. Time of relief - 5 pm to 7.10 pm. Batt'n moved to the following area - BN. H.Q & 'A' Coy to Q. 26. [Sht. 57c] Museum. METZ	

WAR DIARY or INTELLIGENCE SUMMARY

Army Form C. 2118.

Place	Date	Hour	Summary of Events and Information	Remarks and references to Appendices
Dec/1-T 19th (cont)	19/12/17 (cont)		"D" Coy to BARRICADE ROAD. [Rg. NINE WOOD. Special Sh. Ranbot S4c NE + SE] C + B. Coys from D Coy - west, occupying trenches on squares R.7.12 + Q.11 RESERVE.	
	20th		D Coy working up the line on NAVAL TRI-AVENUE - R.g. from 4pm to 8pm.	
	21st		Scaled inspection of A. Coy + B. Coy.	
	22nd		The Barr. billeted in METZ. B.C. + B. Coys being relieved by 2 Coys of 14th WORCESTERS own pioneer battalion. SUB.LIEUT. R. TAYLOR. killed while in charge of advanced party of Coy to Metz.	
	23rd		Enemy aeroplane brought down near Bn HQ. 3.30pm - The wreckage soon surrounded by the NELSONS. Advanced party set off for the line at 6.30 pm - The Batt. arrived at the Drake Bn HQ at 9.10pm - The Batt. frontage sideslipped to the right, own right flank resting at point 400 yds N.W of LA VACQUERIE. NELSONS relieved the Drakes - time of relief 6.0 pm to 10.35 pm	
	24th		Consolidation of trenches - wiring - working on new CT's fire trenches. Patrols -	
	25th		Very quiet all the time in the line. No signs of enemy attack.	
	26th		2nd LIEUT. F.D. PURCER. Snipers & killed while touring the line amongst his men.	
	27th		Men were well fed with hot food - very few casualties with trench feet.	
	28th		Sub. LIEUT. T. WHITE. KILLED with several other ranks gone by shell falling into dugout. Relieved by DRAKES. Time of relief - 5.15pm to 10.45pm. The H⁰'s moved into Bde. Supp‡ occupying trenches on HIGHLAND RIDGE MAP.REF. NINE WOOD 1/10,000 R8a, R2b, R.1.b, R.1.d. BnHQ at R.2.60.35.	

WAR DIARY
INTELLIGENCE SUMMARY

(Erase heading not required.)

Army Form C. 2118.

Place	Date	Hour	Summary of Events and Information	Remarks and references to Appendices
HIGHLAND RIDGE. F. NINE WOOD. 1/10,000. SHT. 57c.	29/12/17		Reconnaissance made of Dugouts in Sector area occupied by Batn. Three found — all with one entrance. C & D Coys working on NAVAL RESERVE. [R.9. NINE WOOD.] 1 from 4.p.m. to 8.p.m. party of 20 men working marking dugouts at B`n` H.Q. R.18.6.89. from 11.30 a.m. to 7.30 p.m. This party is to work until Dugouts are completed. HIGHLAND RIDGE shelled during night by 5.9" & 30" SUB. LIEUT. M. BOYS — wounded.	
OPERATIONS COUNTER ATTACK.	30/31st	6.30 a.m. [Bat n] 7.25 a.m. 10.25 a.m. 2.15 p.m.	A heavy enemy barrage was laid by enemy apparently on whole of Divisional front. Orders received to reinforce the DRAKES with one Coy. The enemy had penetrated our front line system of trenches but for the time was held up by the Drakes. Orders received from Bde to man NAVAL RESERVE with remainder of Batt`n` B`n` H.Q. being in Ravine at R.8.c.9.o. Completed by 2.30 p.m. In accordance with orders from O.C. Drakes. C Coy (Nelson) counterattacked for WELSH SUPPORT. R.15.a.8s.70 to R.9.b.46.00. from NAVAL R. over the top — No artillery barrage. Our men succeeded in gaining objective, but the right was held up by machine gunfire. At the same time a bombing party bombed up FARM. AVE. at R.15.a.6.9. towards the right end of WELSH SUPPORT, meeting considerable opposition. SPLENDID GALLANTRY was shown by SUB LIEUT. CLERK. O.C. C Coy.	

WAR DIARY
INTELLIGENCE SUMMARY

Army Form C. 2118.

Place	Date	Hour	Summary of Events and Information	Remarks and references to Appendices
OPERATIONS COUNTER ATTACK. (CONT.)	30/12/17.		who, although severely wounded did not relinquish his command until forced to do so through weakness + loss of blood. Petty Officer J.C. WINN. who was in charge of the bombing party Medway also showed splendid gallantry during the attack.	
		4pm.	Orders No. 142. received from Bde.	
		4.30pm	In accordance with the above orders 'A' Coy (OC LIEUT. W.D. WELLWOOD) on the right supported by D. Coy. (OC LIEUT. L. SPAIN) attacked at 4.30 p.m. from NAVAL RESERVE. B Coy (OC LIEUT H.B. BIGGS) in cooperation with the Drakes on the left attacked on the immediate left. The attack was entirely successful, WELSH SUPPORT reoccupied, and by 5.30 p.m. after a little bombing on our right we were in touch with one of the companies of the Anson Bn (of the 188th Bde), who had taken part in the attack. During the operations the enemy put down a very heavy barrage on the area between WOOD AVE + FARM M. TR. along NELSON RESERVE. but fortunately we suffered very few casualties. Great initiative + courage was shown by LIEUT. H.B. BIGGS (B Coy). LIEUT. W.D. WELLWOOD (A Coy) and Chief Petty Officer J. MARCHANT. (A Coy)	
		4.30	Two platoons from (B Coy) under SUB. LIEUT. L.C. ANDERSON. were sent to reinforce	

WAR DIARY
or
INTELLIGENCE SUMMARY.

Army Form C. 2118.

Place	Date	Hour	Summary of Events and Information	Remarks and references to Appendices
	30/31/12/17		The left coy of the Drakes. The coolness & devotion to duty of Sub Lieut ANDERSON were outstanding features. The final dispositions of NELSON BATTN on the night of 30th.31st were - WELSH SUPPORT firing line. - C. Coy on the right in touch with the ANSON.Bn.; A Coy centre, two Platoons of A Coy; B Coy Drakes, + 2 Platoons A Coy (NELSON). NAVAL RESERVE was garrisoned by B Coy withdrawn from WELSH SUPPORT.	
		7.30 pm	Food, water and ammunition in ample supplies were carried up to the front line as early as 7.30, by men of D. Coy.	
			The remainder of the night of 30th morning of 31st passed off with intermittent shelling and great activity of enemy TMs, Snipers and machine gun fire. The work of the battalion stretcher bearers during the operations and under cover of darkness enabled us to evacuate all our wounded by 8 am of the 31st. The batts and coy runners' work was wonderful to the extreme. Every message which had to be carried was at certain points in the open where the ground was being constantly swept by shell fire, machine gun and rifle bullets.	

Army Form C. 2118.

WAR DIARY
INTELLIGENCE SUMMARY
(Erase heading not required.)

Instructions regarding War Diaries and Intelligence Summaries are contained in F. S. Regs., Part II. and the Staff Manual respectively. Title pages will be prepared in manuscript.

Place	Date	Hour	Summary of Events and Information	Remarks and references to Appendices
COUNTER ATTACK (CONT.)	30/12/17.		When the three Coys were ordered to man NAVAL RESERVE. LIEUT. T.W. WHITTAKER. DSO. 2nd in command NELSONS and SUB LIEUT H.C. BIRCH proceeded to the Bn HQrs. & thence to NAVAL AVE. to ensure that correct positions were taken up. Their Head Quarters were made at junction of NAVAL & TRENCH. AVE. and they acted as Liaison between NELSONS & DRAKES. The little splendid behaviour of LIEUT. WHITTAKER in the organising and the passing of orders to Coy commanders & in keeping Bn HQ posted as to the condition of affairs during the operations proved of incalculable value. Great gallantry was displayed by LIEUT. HARRIS MC [illeg.] (two stars) officers and other ranks of B Coy Drakes, & their splendid work in the reoccupying of WALSH SUPPORT. Their work is spoken of in the highest terms by all who were in the vicinity. Casualties of NELSON BN during operations of 30/12th :- Officers :- SUB. LIEUT. C.A. CLERK (OC. Coy) [wounded] SUB. LIEUT. H. BENNETT. [do] SUB. LIEUT. T.G. COBURN. [do] Other Ranks :- Approxy 100 - Killed, wounded & missing.	Stuart & Jurs Lt. Colonel Comdg Nelson Bn. R.N.V.R.

WAR DIARY
or
INTELLIGENCE SUMMARY.

(Erase heading not required.)

Army Form C. 2118.

Nelson Bn Vol 20

Place	Date	Hour	Summary of Events and Information	Remarks and references to Appendices
IN THE LINE – LA JACQBERIE SECTOR.	1918. 1/1/18.		[RSF. MAP. 57c. SPECIAL SHEET. "NINE WOOD." 1/10,000.] Very busy Consolidating WELSH SUPPORT. attack of 30/31st Dec. 17. R.9.d. Front line running north from South R.15.a. 85.95 up WELSH SUPPORT. joining WOOD AVE at about R.9.b. 45.00. East along Wood avenue to point R.10.c.15.68 North up NELSON TRENCH to point R.10.a. 30.00. The trench in very bad condition with the late heavy bombardments B^n H.Q at R.9.b. 2.3. The following officers joined the Batt. SUB. LIEUT. W.W. THOMAS. SUB.LIEUT. A.T. ROBERTSON. SUB. LIEUT. BLIVETT. JR. and SUB LIEUT. A.V. DUTTON.	
	2/1/18.		Very quiet in the line. SUB. LIEUT. W.W. THOMAS. Sniped at and wounded.	
	3/1/18		Consolidation still going on. Although the men in the line are heavily taxed physically, the morale & spirits of all are excellent. Hot food is being very well supplied, and the percentage of trench feet very low.	
	4th		Batt relieved by Drake Batt on night of 3rd except C & D Companies which remained in NAVAL RESERVE.	
	5th		The remainder of the batt moved into support on HIGHLAND RIDGE.	
	6th		Batt moved into METZ. Scabies inspection. Batt at METZ.	

Army Form C. 2118.

WAR DIARY
or
INTELLIGENCE SUMMARY.
(Erase heading not required.)

Instructions regarding War Diaries and Intelligence Summaries are contained in F.S. Regs., Part II. and the Staff Manual respectively. Title pages will be prepared in manuscript.

Hour, Date, Place		Summary of Events and Information	Remarks and references to Appendices
Jan. 18.	METZ.	The Batt^n still billeted in METZ.	
8th "	"	The battalion relieved the Bedfords. Times of relief 5.0 pm to 7.30 pm	
9th "	In the line		
10th "	"	Advanced party sent down to HAVRINCOURT WOOD. Q.15.c. to take over from the 4th Bedfords (190.R.Bde) Nelson relieved by the Bedfords. The Nelson Batt^n moved back into Havrincourt Wood A MB. coys arriving about 11 pm the 10th. The remainder of Batt^n arrived in camps about 3. a.m the 11th. 2nd LIEUT. H.B. CANNIN killed while on patrol.	
11th "	NELSON CAMP. [HAVRINCOURT WOOD]	The men busy cleaning clothes & equipment. The camps now occupied, named NELSON CAMP. [Q.15.C.]	
12th "	"	Improving of camp. drainage. duckboarding etc.	
13th "	"	The camp inspected by the Corps General.	
14th "	"	The battalion bathed in METZ.	
15th "	"	All officers reconnoitred the METZ defences.	
16th "	"		
17th "	"	Advanced reconnoitring parties sent up the line.	
18th "	In the line	The Batt^n relieved the 4th Bedfords. front line in very bad condition. Men busy building firing positions + cleaning up to the waist in mud + water at parts.	
19th "	"		

WAR DIARY or INTELLIGENCE SUMMARY

Army Form C. 2118.

(Erase heading not required.)

Hour, Date, Place		Summary of Events and Information	Remarks and references to Appendices
20 Jan 18.	In the line.	Brigadier & Brigade Major round the line. Duckboards now up to the front line for use at dusk. The advance party of Hawke Bn arrived.	
21st	"	Advance party of Nelson away at 12 noon to take over from Hawke Bn in HAVRINCOURT WOOD. Q15 c.9.3. Nelson relieved by Hawke 6 p.m. – 9.15 p.m. The Nelson Bn remained the night in HAVRINCOURT WOOD. NOTE – There was very little sickness new cases of trench feet during this turn in the line, as was expected because of bad state of the trenches.	
22nd	" EQUANCOURT	Relieved by 2nd Bn Ox. & Bucks. Bn moved to EQUANCOURT. relieving the 1st K.S.L.I.	
23rd	" BARASTRE AREA.	The Bn entrained in light train at 3.0 p.m. for ROCQUIGNY. arriving there at 5.5 p.m. Marched to BARASTRE AREA. taking over from the 23rd Royal Fusiliers, in Camp at O.10.c.3.9. SHEET. 57c. S.W. 1/40,000.	
24th	" "	The camp reorganised & disposition map sent to Brigade.	
25th	" "	The 2nd in command adjutant and half Batt. officers reconnoitred the HERMIES rear defences.	
26th	" "	The Co. & remainder of the officers reconnoitred area as yesterday.	
27th	" "	Rifle ranges inspected necessary material for repair & improvement indented for.	
28th	" "	Bn on parade during morning.	

Army Form C. 2118.

WAR DIARY
or
INTELLIGENCE SUMMARY.
(Erase heading not required.)

Instructions regarding War Diaries and Intelligence Summaries are contained in F. S. Regs., Part II. and the Staff Manual respectively. Title pages will be prepared in manuscript.

Hour, Date, Place	Summary of Events and Information	Remarks and references to Appendices
29th Jan 18. BARASTRE AREA.	Earthwork round all huts against enemy bombing in progress. Similar breastworks being built round the horse standings.	
30th " CAMP O.10.c.39. Ref Sh 57c S.E. 1/40,000	Rifle ranges & bayonet course being repaired & earthwork round huts & at transport lines continued.	
31st " "	Bn Training during morning. Breastworks in camp, cleaned & raised. Improvements on rifle ranges & bayonet course continued.	

Stuart E. Jones
Commdr RNVR
Comdg NELSON Battn.

(73989) W4141—463. 400,000. 9/14. H.&J.,Ltd. Forms/C. 2118/10.

CONFIDENTIAL

HEADQUARTERS.
NELSON Bn.

FINAL WAR DIARY

of the

NELSON BATTALION

from

1st February, 1918

To

25th February, 1918

To H.Q's
63rd (R.N.) Division

Stuart E. Jones
Cmdr R.N.V.R
Cmdg NELSON Bn

Vol 21
Closed

WAR DIARY or INTELLIGENCE SUMMARY

Army Form C. 2118.

Hour, Date, Place	Summary of Events and Information	Remarks and references to Appendices
1st February 1918. BARASTRE AREA CAMP O.10.c.3.9. Ref. Sht. 57 C. S.W. 1/40,000.	Training according to programme 6.15 A.M. to 12.30 P.M. and 2 to 3.30 P.M. Working parties moving up Pack tanks round Staircases in Transport lines.	
2nd	Battalion allotted Baths. Companies to Inspection.	
3rd	Church Parade. Specialists Wiring Instruction.	
4th	Training & programme. "A" Coy at LE TRANSLOY range. Working parties building Range and throwing up Earthworks round Stablings in Transport Lines.	
5th	Batt: Parade at 7-15 a.m. Programme 169 "B" Coy are 3 pots with Battalion Rifles. Rest Pl 1 to 1½ broken up, men received arrears of pay of August deficiencies in kit made. Working party of 300 O.R. under 2/Lt Forward proceeded to HAVRINCOURT WOOD and worked on dugouts explosive at Q.15.a.6.6., G.O.C. Division inspected work during forenoon. Training as per programme 8.15 a.m. to 12.20 and 2 to 3.0 p.m.	
6th	Working party of 150 O.R. under 2/Lt "B" Coy proceeded by bus to Q.15.a.6.6. Remainder of Battalion cleaning up and getting ready to train. At 3.0 p.m. the following detail Lt Col Maird O.C., Lt Col Woodcock 2/Lt Hardy 2/Lt Welling 10 off and 200 O.R. 1/7th DRAKE. 3 officers 100 O.R. 16/1002 O.Z. 4860 A. B.) Boots, has been attached Lowis as Course (321 & 6 Bn.) Working party of 150 O.R. under Ot "B" Coy proceeded by bus to Q.15.a.6.6. Inspection of Transport.	
7th	Training on programme 8.15 a.m. 12 - 3.30 p.m. Voluntary Church Service.	
8th		
9th	Musketry Training. Firing practice at 200 yds on LE TRANSLOY range.	25 yds range by Brigade.
10th		at 116.
11th		Lt Col Smith O.C. Doing Lt. Col No. E. HEARD appointed M.O. ½ of Nelson Batt.
12th		
13th	In Transport to FORESTS 193rd Brigade	

WAR DIARY or INTELLIGENCE SUMMARY

Army Form C. 2118.

Hour, Date, Place	Summary of Events and Information	Remarks and references to Appendices
4th February 1918. BAPAUME AREA	Truard to WIMTERA Camp	
"	Shooting Competition in Returning.	
"	50 O.R. marched off at 8.0 am. to D.M.O working party. Would Brigade.	
"	3 Officers and 100 O.Rs at 12.45 p.m. for work under D.T.M.O. in HAVRINCOURT WOOD (D.7.d.)	
"	Artillery Camp in Brigade Camp giving up certain huts to 9th Cheshires. A/K No Bdge Brigade. 50 O.R. and 70 NEUVILLE as working party for D.M.G.O.	
"	50 O.R. returned from NEUVILLE. 100 O.Rs sent to METZ Camp (9 ng a2) H.O.Rs. Sent to YTRES Camp (P20b)	
"	Received orders (63"Div) H25D/3/A dated 20/2/18 for transport of all officers available and 489 O.R. to 16 Infantry Batt.	
"	100 O.Rs sent 2 officers returning from HAVRINCOURT WOOD. 50 OTR: returned from DTD. 21 ORs from METZ & YTRES Camp. Nominal rolls prepared for Transport. 10 - 15 17th Infantry Batt.	
"	Transferred 8 Officers and 445 O.Rs. 16 J 17 Battalion Batt. The remainder viz 3 officers and 23 Ors. moved to NEAPARA Camp at - RUYAULCAUAT (P10b)	
"	Battalion Supplies viz 3 officers and 23 O.R's moved to Inf. Brigade Headquarters in RUYAULCAOULT awaiting final disposal. Battalion totally disbanded. WAR DIARY CLOSED.	